Articles, Essays & Notes

HARDWICK MUSING

Terry Kilburn

Terry Kilburn (signature)

... dedicated to those who are open to alternative ideas,
who are prepared to take on board new facts and theories and
are ready and willing to adapt to changing narratives.

Written & Compiled by Terry Kilburn © 2020
Chapter 3 Written by Helen Wyld & Terry Kilburn

© All rights reserved. No part of this publication may be reproduced, stored in a retrieval system, or transmitted in any form or by any means electronic, mechanical, photocopied, recorded or otherwise, without the prior written permission of the publisher and copyright holder.
All pictures, drawings, diagrams, names or trademarks are copyright their respective owners.

The contents of this book are believed correct at the time of printing. Nevertheless, the publishers can not be held responsible for any errors, omissions or for changes in the details given in this book or for the consequences of any reliance on the information provided by the same.
This does not affect your statutory rights.

Front Cover Photograph: Hardwick Hall - Alastair Wallace /Shutterstock
Cover Design: Christopher Trousdale /Ammonite Creative
Back Cover: Needlework Embroidery, Hardwick Hall - Robert Thrift /National Trust
Inner Cover Photograph: Hardwick Hall Turret - Terry Kilburn

First Published: 2020
Second Impression: 2020

ISBN: 978 0 9566147 5 9

Published by **Jetprint**

(Jetprint is a trading name of Vassalli Limited, Y022 4NQ. Company Reg. No. 7159214)
www.jetprintwhitby.co.uk

Printed and bound in the U.K.

Extract from a nineteenth century transcript of the
Memorandum of Arthur Mower (d. 1610)
Woolley collection Brit Mus Add Mss 6671

"The old Countess of Shrewsbury departed forth of this world the Saturday being the 13th day of February at Hardwick and was carried to Derby of Tuesday the next after to her tomb there in All Hallows Church and there buried anno dom. 1607* in the fifth year of our most dread Lord King James – who was in her time a great purchaser and getter together of much lands and much goods, and was first married to Robert Barley of Barley esq. and then to William Cavendish knight, and then to William Southlow (St Loo) knight captain of the guards, and last to George Talbot, Earl of Shrewsbury who did surmount her name. She builed Chattesworth, Hardwick, Owlcotts and was a great builder and purchaser."

*Old Style, 1608 New Style.

Articles, Essays & Notes
HARDWICK MUSING

Contents   *Page*

Introduction 1

1. The Marriage and Wardship of Robert Barley,
   First Husband of Bess of Hardwick 5

2. Sir William Cavendish, Marriage to Bess
   and Relocation to Derbyshire 31

3. Hardwick's Sabine Tapestries 57

4. Three Into Two Won't Go: Marriage
   and Hardwick's 'Eglantine Table' 69

5. Matters of Birth and Death 75

6. The Marmion Connection 89

7. Hardwick's Royal Princess: Lady Arbella Stuart 117

Epilogue: My Bess 131

Introduction

Between 2012 and 2015 I was a National Trust volunteer at Derbyshire's Hardwick Hall. During these four seasons I was a room guide and tour guide and met some interesting and wonderful characters among my fellow volunteers. I learned a lot from them. Late Spring and Summer saw hundreds of visitors to Hardwick's New Hall and some visitors even took the time to wander around the remains of the Old Hall in the care of English Heritage. The number of visitors to Hardwick naturally ebbed and flowed according to the season. Late Spring and Summer kept 'mansion' volunteers very busy, even when much of the time was spent on 'traffic duty' ensuring that visitors followed the designated route. Early and late season, say, up to Easter and from late September, the volume of visitors naturally dwindled. I think all volunteers enjoyed their inter-actions with members of the public, some of whom were very knowledgeable, other less so.

On quiet days I would spend a good deal of my time pondering everything that was around me, peeping into every nook and cranny discovering things that I found intriguing. In the Long Gallery, for example, I came across graffiti scratched into the stone blocks that make up the great fireplaces. My favourite find was the name Claire Derrie. In the eighteenth century the Derrys were landlords of the near-by Hardwick Inn. Another example was the wall painting hidden behind tapestries on the south wall of the State Withdrawing Room that once stretched right up to the coving of the original ceiling before it was lowered to create rooms above. The jury is still out as to whether the band of undressed stonework around the exterior of the hall is evidence of the original loggia being unfinished or of its seventeenth century removal. Many more examples could be cited.

My training as a historian told me that some of the things said to the general public somehow didn't add up. I expressed my concerns to one of my friends and mentors, an Emeritus Professor, who replied he had visited many National Trust properties and that in his experience most volunteers were "well-meaning" but were not necessarily historians. I came across many well-meaning volunteers at Hardwick. Few consulted academic journals. Most gleaned their knowledge by reading two relatively recent biographies of Bess: David Durant's *Bess of Hardwick: Portrait of an Elizabethan Dynast* first published in 1977 and Mary S Lovell's *Bess of Hardwick: First Lady of Chatsworth* first published in 2005. Both books are well-written and informative, recommended reading for anyone with an interest in Bess of Hardwick.

The first two chapters here are based upon articles published by the Derbyshire Archaeological Society. 'The Marriage and Wardship of Robert Barley …' was published in the *Derbyshire Archaeological Journal* (Vol 134, 2014). A short 'Addendum' to this article was published in 2016 (Vol 136). Here these two articles are combined and additional documents appended including a transcript of Bess's 1546 complaint to Chancery. The discovery of new documentary evidence enabled me to revise what is known about Bess's first marriage to Robert Barley and draw attention to the previously unknown role played by Peter Freschevile in Robert's wardship and marriage together with the consequences this had for Bess as she sought to pursue her claims for dower. At the time they were writing neither Durant nor Lovell were aware of the role of Peter Freschevile in Robert Barley's wardship and his marriage to Bess and consequently there is no mention of this in their books.

My article 'Sir William Cavendish: Marriage to Bess …' was published in the *Derbyshire Archaeological Journal* (Vol 139, 2019). By placing his actions in the context of the political and religious upheavals of the mid-sixteenth century, the article seeks to provide new explanations for Sir William's marriage to Bess and move to Derbyshire.

The notes on Hardwick's Romulus and Titus Tatius tapestry, one of four tapestries or parts thereof at Hardwick, was co-written with Dr Helen Wyld and are taken directly from the National Trust's Collections website. I was also able to identify three other tapestries belonging to this 'Sabine' series. As a result of our work, Hardwick's Sabine tapestries have been given high priority for preservation by the National Trust.

INTRODUCTION

'Three Into Two Won't Go…' was published in the Derbyshire Archaeological Society's *Derbyshire Miscellany* (Vol 21: Part 2, 2016) and seeks to show that Hardwick's famous 'Eglantine Table' does not represent three marriages.

Bess's story is somewhat bedevilled by inaccuracy and myth. Recent years have seen some confusion emerge over the year of Bess's birth. Was she born in 1521/2 or 1527? Is 1527 a modern myth? Another Hardwick myth is that Bess's corpse lay in state in the High Great Chamber for some three months before her funeral was held at Derby. Very early in my four-season stint as a volunteer at Hardwick I was told by a long-time volunteer that this was because Bess died in February when the winter weather was not conducive for a ceremonial burial and so her corpse was placed in a lead coffin in the High Great Chamber. There it remained until the arrival of more clement weather in May. Amazingly, this story was repeated as recently as 2018 by a prominent celebrity historian in a popular history magazine. The evidence we have tells a very different story.

In 2014 the National Trust came up with one of its better ideas and chose to focus the attention of visitors to Hardwick on the story of Bess's granddaughter, Arbella Stuart. Volunteers set about reading David Durant's 1978 *Arbella Stuart: A Rival to the Queen* and perhaps Sarah Gristwood's 2003 *Arbella: England's Lost Queen*. It is doubtful many skimmed through Ruth Norrington's *In the Shadow of the Throne* (2002). It occurred to me that a 'quick fix' was needed and so I set about writing a brief self-published biography of Arbella, *Hardwick's Royal Princess…*, which is reproduced in this book.

Henry Marmion appeared to me to be a shadowy figure closely associated with the Hardwicks. The Marmion Connection seeks to explore this relationship further. The book ends with an epilogue: an assessment of my Bess.

Printed in a very small run, the main purpose of this book is to bring together in a single volume some of my published research, views and conclusions, on various Hardwick topics. The reader is asked to remember that the chapters were written at different times and may therefore appear to contain contradictions and some degree of repetition. This book is intended as a work of reference. It is perhaps understandable that new ideas meet resistance. It can be hard to accept something that challenges what we think we know. For some, the easy way out is to seek comfort in the notion that unless what is said concurs with better-known authors it can readily be dismissed. Some will find elements of the book challenging, perhaps controversial, even heretical, but my hope is that it will in some small way help to eliminate some of the mythology and inaccuracies that continue to distort the Bess of Hardwick narrative. The work is dedicated to those Hardwick volunteers who are open to alternative ideas, who are prepared to take onboard new facts and theories and who are ready and willing to adapt to changing narratives.

Academic journals tend not to favour long and detailed footnotes. I have chosen to include detailed footnotes where appropriate as they contain a good deal of useful additional information to that included in the main text. On the other hand, I have not included a lengthy reading list although many printed and documentary sources are cited in footnotes together with unpublished primary material. I have eschewed an index.

Finally, I acknowledge the contributions of the following people who, one way or another, have influenced the work published in this book: Philip Riden, Peter Foden, Jonathan Mackman, Lesley Bilby, Maureen Taylor and Paul Gliddon. My thanks are extended to staff at the University of Nottingham Manuscripts and Special Collections and the Borthwick Institute for Archives at York University. Errors that remain are of my own making.

Terry Kilburn
Stainsacre, March 2020

1

The Wardship and Marriage of Robert Barley, First Husband of Bess of Hardwick

In 2010 Philip Riden published an account of the Hardwick family of Hardwick Hall during the fifteenth and sixteenth centuries.[1] One of the questions he examined was the first of the four marriages of Elizabeth Hardwick, better known to history as 'Bess of Hardwick'. Riden showed that much of the traditional account of how Bess met her first husband, Robert Barley, is at best fanciful. Although David Durant repeated the traditional account, he was the first to suggest that Robert's marriage to Bess was an arrangement made to mitigate the impact of wardship on the Barley estate.[2]

Robert's father, Arthur Barley, had substantial debts even before he entered into his inheritance on the death of his father in 1533. A writ was issued against him in November 1530 for the sum of £100 which he owed to James Daniel, a London merchant taylor.[3] Marriage in the sixteenth century was often considered to be little more than a business transaction, a commodity to be bought and sold. It is possible that his debts led Arthur to sell Robert's marriage and wardship in the 1530s rather than any pressing need to stave off the Court of Wards. Sometime between 1533 and 1538 Arthur sold Robert's wardship and marriage to Bess's stepfather, Ralph Leche. At some date no later than 1538 Ralph's debts led him to sell Robert's wardship and marriage to Henry Marmion. After Arthur's death, some of his lands were deemed to be held by knight service to the king. This led to Godfrey Boswell's purchase of Robert's wardship.[4] Robert was aged 13 when his father died on 28 May 1543. The exact date of Robert's marriage to Bess is not known though it is thought to have taken place in the spring of that year.[5] If so, it was destined to be of short duration. Robert died in December 1544.[6]

A chance discovery among recently digitized legal records at the National Archives has brought to light new evidence which adds significantly to our understanding of Robert Barley's wardship and marriage.[7] The document is an attachment relating to a plea submitted by an attorney acting on behalf of Peter Freschevile of Staveley. Dating from late 1543 or early 1544, it requires the sheriff to attach certain persons who were to appear before the judges in the Court of Common Pleas at Easter 1544, and clearly relates to proceedings begun by Freschevile shortly after Robert's marriage to Bess and the death of Arthur Barley.[8] It would have been one of a series of entries relating to the case which alleged trespass and abduction. Freschevile claimed that Ralph Leche, Elizabeth his wife, and Henry Marmion '…with force and arms they did take and abduct Robert Barley, having been found at Barley, the son and heir of Arthur Barley Esquire, being under-age, whose marriage belongs to this Peter, against the will of this Peter.' Bess's mother was first cousin to Peter Freschevile's mother, both women sharing the maiden name, Elizabeth Leake.[9] Ralph Leche married Bess's widowed mother in or about 1529.[10] The sheriff was also ordered to find Robert and place him in his safe keeping until the court determined to whom he was to be returned. Durant and others cite evidence from the Court of Wards to argue that Robert and Bess were married shortly before Arthur Barley's death. When Boswell acquired Robert's wardship it was stated that Robert was married in his father's lifetime.[11]

The Frescheviles claimed that the Barleys held the manor of Barlow by knight service of their manor of Staveley and that therefore they - the Frescheviles - held the rights of wardship and marriage should Barlow be inherited by an under-age heir.[12] The Barleys believed they held Barlow by socage and could therefore dispose of Robert's wardship and marriage as they chose. As far as the Frescheviles were concerned, Robert's wardship and marriage were not the Barleys to sell. Peter Freschevile has not previously been associated with Robert Barley's wardship and marriage, yet it is clear from his Common Pleas action that he considered himself to be Robert's lawful guardian and sought confirmation of this. By 1538 Arthur Barley had sold Robert's wardship and marriage to Ralph Leche. In a Chancery bill dateable to no later than 1538, during a period in which Ralph was under pressure of debt, Henry Marmion stated that he had paid Ralph Leche £41 9s. 2d. for Robert's wardship and marriage.[13] In terms of common law, being of age meant being 21 or over. Freschevile stated that Robert was under-age but did not comment on Bess's age. Robert was born in January 1530 and so in 1538 would have been about eight years of age. When it came to marriage canon law held that boys were supposed to be at least 14 years of age. On the other hand, Bess, born in 1521 or 1522, would have been in her mid-teens and would have been considered 'of age' in terms of eligibility for marriage.[14] Marmion would have claimed still to hold Robert's wardship at the time of Robert's marriage to Bess which probably explains why he was included in Freschevile's allegations of trespass and abduction.

Although Robert's wardship and marriage appear to have been sold twice by 1538 it was not until 1543, shortly after Arthur Barley's death and Robert's marriage to Bess, that Freschevile commenced proceedings alleging that force had been used to abduct Robert. He claimed that Robert's marriage to Bess was illegal because he, as Robert's lawful guardian, had not consented to it. He clearly looked upon the marriage as a deliberate attempt to deprive him of his rights to Robert's wardship and with it control of the Barley inheritance during Robert's minority and perhaps longer. A marriage achieved by force was invalid and this is probably the reason Freschevile alleged that Robert had been abducted, and by implication, married under duress.[15] After Robert's death Freschevile became the lawful guardian of Robert's younger brother and heir, George Barley, who was thereafter married to Freschevile's daughter, Jane.[16] It is possible that Jane had been intended to marry Robert. If so, his marriage to Bess threatened to thwart Freschevile's ambitions and resulted in his taking action to uphold his rights as Robert's lawful guardian.

Plaintiffs and defendants almost habitually exaggerated the arguments that they or their attorneys put before the courts. Robert was taken in order to secure possession of his person and it is possible that in order to strengthen his case Freschevile exaggerated his claim that he had been removed by force of arms. However, even allowing for a degree of exaggeration, Freschevile's allegations cannot be dismissed out of hand. Ralph Leche and Henry Marmion were variously accused in other legal actions in which the use of arms may have been involved. Among his many dubious dealings Ralph was accused leading an assault on cattle in Mackworth. James Hardwick's guardian, John Bugby, was allegedly thrown out of Hardwick Hall by John Hardwick's executors, Henry Marmion and John Leake, in what was described as a violent assault on the property and in 1540/1 Marmion appears to have masterminded an alleged attack at Chatsworth for which he, Bess's mother and others, were brought before the Derby assizes and later investigated by Star Chamber.[17]

At the very least Freschevile was challenging a marriage that certainly took place and his allegations do demonstrate the lengths to which plaintiffs might go to support their cases in the courts. It remains unclear whether Freschevile was claiming that Robert had been kidnapped from an actual building, possibly the Barley's home at Barlow Lees which Ralph claimed to have purchased along with Robert's wardship, or whether the reference to Robert 'having been found at Barley' referred simply to the manor of Barlow. It is also unclear whether Freschevile's proceedings were solely concerned with the violation of what he took to be his rights as the Barley family's feudal overlord or whether they were rooted in a struggle for control not only of Robert's marriage but also his inheritance. Despite being encumbered with various debts and two claims for dower, this included land, timber, fishponds, coal, ironstone, smithies and bloomeries.[18]

Arthur Barley's widow, Elizabeth, sued for her dower but was unable to name Robert's guardian. Following Robert's death in December 1544 Freschevile became George Barley's guardian and in early 1545 promptly accepted her claim for dower without challenge.[19] It was at this time that in order to establish her legal rights to dower in the Barley estate Bess sued Freschevile and his ward George Barley in the Court of Common Pleas. However, Freschevile continued to maintain his belief that Bess's marriage to Robert had been illegal and he denied Bess's claim for dower. During 1545 two writs of dower were issued by the Court of Common Pleas to which after some prevarication Freschevile now claimed that Robert had never been seised of the estate from which Bess was seeking dower. She answered that Freschevile's claim was untrue and intended simply to "delay and fatigue" her dower proceeding. She stated that she had been without "friends, aid or comfort," that her stepfather, Ralph Leche, possibly then in the Fleet prison, stood "condemned of great sums of money" and that neither she nor her mother could afford to continue to try the issue at Common Law. Early in 1546 Freschevile engaged Sir John Chaworth, Robert's uncle, to offer Bess an out-of-court settlement which she later argued was proof of her entitlement to dower. Freschevile offered to withdraw his claim and pay Bess dower providing she agreed to farm out her widow's third at an annual rent. Bess, "enforced thereunto by necessity", accepted the advice of her counsel and agreed to these terms. She estimated the value of her dower at £26 13s 4d (i.e., the 40 marks marriage portion left to her in her father's will). Chaworth offered only £16. Bess "constrained by necessity than compelled by equity" reluctantly accepted Chaworth's offer but at the eleventh-hour Freschevile reneged on the agreement determining instead to continue with his claim in the Court of Common Pleas. It was now, some eighteen months since Robert's death, that Bess turned to the equity courts and commenced proceedings against Freschevile and George Barley in the Court of Chancery.

Bess's Common Pleas and Chancery actions were as much concerned with the legality of her marriage as they were about her dower. In her initial complaint to Chancery addressed to the Lord Chancellor, Sir Thomas Wriothesley, Bess explained how her marriage to Robert had come about. She was at pains to demonstrate that her marriage to Robert was lawful and, as had already been recorded in the Court of Wards, that it had taken place before the death of Robert's father. Bess informed Chancery that Arthur did "covenant and bargain" and had been paid 'diverse great sums of money' for her marriage to Robert. It has been assumed that these events took place in 1543 but Bess did not state when they had taken place. Her sole reference to 1543 was in relation to Robert's inheritance on the death of his father. It seems probable that Ralph Leche had in mind a marriage with Bess when he first purchased Robert's wardship and marriage from Arthur Barley some years before 1543 and that this remained the intention when Ralph sold on Robert's wardship and marriage to Henry Marmion. It is reasonable to assume that Arthur had been paid for Robert's wardship and marriage when Ralph Leche had purchased them and that "being then but of tender years" Robert and Bess were espoused at that time but Robert was too young to consummate the marriage. [20]

Bess informed Chancery that various payments had been made to Arthur Barley but it is unclear who had actually made them.[21] She may have been referring to the monies paid for Robert's wardship and marriage by Ralph and Henry Marmion. Riden has demonstrated the precarious nature of Ralph's finances.[22] In 1537 Ralph was sued for debt in the Court of Common Pleas by Sir John Byron. Byron sued again the following year when Ralph was amongst defendants facing proceedings for debt commenced by Henry

Bird, a Yeoman of the Chamber.[23] In 1538 Bess's mother accused Ralph of desertion and leaving her and the children Ralph had fathered by her on the verge of destitution, dependent on the charity of friends and neighbours.[24] An undated Star Chamber account refers to legal process in the London Guildhall regarding the administration of a case before the mayoral court between July and October 1538 brought by Ralph against Arthur Barley relating to the recovery of a debt of 100 marks. The nature of the debt is not given but Arthur lost the case and was imprisoned in London's Poultry Compter. The writ by which he was imprisoned, dated the 4th of July 1538, stated that he should remain in prison until he had paid Ralph the 100 marks plus £3 damages. However, on the 17th of July, William Pickering, an attorney acting on behalf of a Ralph Aleyn, alleged that Ralph owed Aleyn a debt of £103. Aleyn claimed that on the 1st of April 1534, in the parish of St Christopher in Cheap ward, London, by a bill of obligation sealed with his seal and presented to the court, Leche acknowledged that he owed Aleyn £200, payable at Pentecost in the following year - 24th May 1535 - but thus far Ralph had only paid £97 and had refused several requests to pay the balance of £103. Summonses were issued requiring Ralph to appear before the mayoral court to answer Aleyn's plea but he failed to do so. On the 6th of October 1538, in accordance with the custom of the city of London, it was ordered that the £69 3s 4d owed to Ralph by Arthur Barley should be paid to Ralph Aleyn as partial repayment of the outstanding £103 owed to him thus leaving Leche to find the remaining balance of £30 6s 8d of his debt to Aleyn.[25] Bess herself referred to Ralph's heavy debts in her dower proceedings and he was to spend time in the Fleet prison in 1538 and again in the mid-1540s, the latter partly in consequence of a long-running dispute with Henry Sacheverell and Dame Elizabeth Savage which included accusations of debt, theft and forgery.[26]

Perhaps aware of his own nearness to death and the need to minimise the impact that wardship would have on his family and estates, Arthur Barley eventually sought to arrange Robert's marriage. Bess did not inform Chancery of the date of her marriage to Robert although her initial complaint to the court clearly indicates that it took place before Arthur Barley's death. There is, however, no evidence that Robert and Bess ever lived together as man and wife. Robert was just short of his fifteenth birthday when he died in December 1544. The main beneficiary of his death was undoubtedly Peter Freschevile as it ensured there would be no heir from the marriage to Bess. As the guardian of Robert's heir George Barley, Freschevile gained what he had wanted. Freschevile's interest in Robert's wardship ended when Robert died but, having lost the Barley wardship once, Freschevile was determined not to lose it a second time. There was to be no challenge to his wardship of George Barley which he claimed as 'lord of the fee', the basis on which he had previously asserted his rights to Robert's wardship.[27] Robert's death would also have brought to an end Freschevile's legal proceedings against Robert's marriage and led to Bess's attempts to secure her widow's dower.

The chance discovery of part of Peter Freschevile's 1543-4 Court of Common Pleas proceedings against Ralph Leche, Elizabeth his wife, and Henry Marmion, sheds new light on the wardship and marriage of Robert Barley. Freschevile's allegations of trespass and the forcible abduction of Robert Barley may have been no more than legal fiction, since he certainly had ample motive to lie to the courts, but his previously unknown involvement in Robert's wardship and marriage adds a new dimension to the narrative. For the first time, we can place Peter Freschevile at the centre of the events and in consequence offer a revised interpretation of Robert's marriage to Bess of Hardwick.

REFERENCES & NOTES:

[1] P. Riden. 'The Hardwicks of Hardwick Hall in the Fifteenth and Sixteenth Centuries', *Derbyshire Archaeological Journal*, 130 (2010), 142 – 75. I am grateful to Philip Riden and Maureen Taylor for helpful comments during the writing of this article.

[2] D. Durant, *Bess of Hardwick: Portrait of an Elizabethan Dynast* (1999), 8 – 11. The assertion that Bess had been in service to the Zouches of Codnor comes from Nathaniel Johnson who in 1692 claimed he had been told by some "ancient gentlemen" that Bess met Robert Barley when she was in service to an otherwise unidentified "Lady Zouche" in London where Robert, also in service to Johnson's Lady Zouche, was lying sick. There were two Lady Zouches resident at Codnor at that time, Lady Margaret Zouche and her daughter-in-law, Lady Anne Zouche. In fact, there is not a single shred of contemporary evidence to indicate that Bess or Robert were ever in service to the Zouches and neither Bess nor Robert Barley were in London when their marriage took place. Johnson also repeated Sir William Dugdale's claim that Robert had left Bess all his lands and thereby she became a wealthy widow, W. Dugdale, *Baronage of England*, 1675, ii, 420-2. This also has no historical foundation. Robert's estate was inherited by his brother, George. Given that Robert's mother and grandmother were also entitled to dower from the estate, Bess could only claim one-third of a window's third (i.e., one-ninth), Riden, 'The Hardwicks', 152, 169. Bess herself estimated her dower entitlement as £26 13s 4d whereas Sir John Chaworth, acting as arbiter, valued it at £16, see Appendix 6. Suffice it to say that Bess certainly did not become a wealthy widow on Robert's death. Writing well over a century and more after the events both Johnson and Dugdale faced an almost complete lack of evidence of Bess's early years. Confronted with the need to explain how a woman of relatively modest birth became a wealthy countess, between them Dugdale and Johnson produced a plausible story which, not surprisingly, went unchallenged at the time and came to be rehashed as fact in the writings of later authors.

[3] The National Archives (TNA), C 241/282/103.

[4] Henry Marmion and John Leake were the executors of the will of Bess's father, John Hardwick. TNA C 1/860/14-15 cited by Riden, 'The Hardwicks',

151-3 and n. 72, 169, is a Chancery case commenced at some point between 1533 and 1538 by Henry Marmion against Ralph Leche, Richard Penniston and William Curtenhall. Marmion claimed the rent of Lees Hall which had been sold with the wardship and marriage of Robert, son and heir apparent of Arthur Barley. TNA C 1/860/14-15 states that 'Arthur Barley, esquire, sold the wardship and marriage of one Robert Barley, his son and heir apparent, to one Rauf Leyche, esquire' (that bit is interlined, but perfectly clear), and then enfeoffed certain lands in Derbyshire worth £10 4d to others, to the use of Ralph who in great debt then sold the marriage, wardship and keeping of the lands to Marmion for £41 9s 2d. These proceedings took place during the chancellorship of Sir Thomas Audley who was Lord Chancellor between 1532 and 1544 but after his elevation in 1538 would have been addressed as Baron or Lord Audley. On Boswell, *aka* Bosvile, see Durant, *Bess*, 10, where he states that at some point after Arthur Barley's death, and before the death of Robert, Robert's wardship was sold for 100 to Bess's brother-in-law, Godfrey Boswell, but Durant does not say from whom Boswell made the purchase. It was, in fact, purchased from the crown. TNA, WARD 7/1/66 (no.164), following Arthur Barley's death Chancery issued a writ for an Inquisition Post-Mortem held at Bolsover on the 12th of October 1543. Among other items, the jurors found Arthur held his lands at Barley Lees by knight service to the king and had left an heir within age. In the case of inheritance this meant under 21. Chancery would have been informed and would have alerted the Court of Wards. The wardship was then sold in the usual way. TNA, WARD 9/152 spans the period 22 April 1539 - 21 April 1546. The Court of Wards record of the sale states that Robert was fourteen years old. Robert was born in January 1530 and therefore Boswell must have made the purchase in 1544. See appendix 3. Boswell entered into his inheritance on the death of his father in 1542. He married Bess's sister, Jane [*aka* Joan] who is described as Boswell's wife in a Court of Common Pleas case begun in 1545/6 by Sir James Foljambe. TNA, CP40/1124 (AALT IMG f346 and IMG f924).

[5] Riden, 'The Hardwicks', 151-2 and nn 72-3, citing TNA, C 142/282/103.

[6] Riden, 'The Hardwicks', 169. Under Canon Law, a marriage between a boy over the age of 14 and a girl over the age of 12 could not be dissolved because it could be consummated. Child marriages, on the other hand, could be and often were dissolved. Thirteen years old in January 1543, Robert was under

the age of 14 when his marriage to Bess took place and, therefore, potentially under Canon Law, the marriage could have been dissolved.

[7] Over eight million images from several classes of medieval and early modern legal records at the National Archives have been digitized by the University of Houston's O'Quinn Law Library. The Anglo-American Legal Tradition digital archive assembled by Robert C. Palmer, Elspeth K.Palmer and Susanne Jenks is available at http://aalt.law.uh.edu/aalt.html (AALT)

[8] TNA, CP 40/1120 (AALT IMG 7469); see appendix 1. I am grateful to Peter Foden for the translation of the original Latin text of appendix 1 and 2.

[9] Peter Freschevile's mother was the daughter of John Leake and Elizabeth Savage. Bess's mother was the daughter of Thomas Leake and Margaret Fox. John and Thomas were the sons of William Leake of Sutton and Katherine Chaworth. 'Pedigree of the Freschevile and Musard Families', *Collectanea Topographica et Genealogica*, 4, (1837), 4; In a box labelled 'pedigrees' in Belvoir Castle Muniments is a book of manuscript pedigrees of landed families *c*.1565. The unknown genealogist was trying to explain contemporary allegiances. Among the hand-drawn pedigrees is one titled 'Leeke Grey and Frechvyle' which includes the marriage of Elizabeth Leake to John Freschevile.

[10] Riden,'The Hardwicks', 153

[11] TNA, WARD 9/152, see appendix 3. Although there is no suggestion that Robert had married anyone else, this document doesn't say who Robert married. The statement that Robert had married before the death of his father is commonly cited as evidence that Robert and Bess were married prior to Arthur Barley's death. However, such a statement had a particular relevance in cases of wardship because the impact of wardship was greater in cases where an under-age heir was unmarried. The statement that Robert had married in the lifetime of his father may have been added simply to reduce the impact of wardship and may not be reliable evidence of the date of Robert's marriage to Bess. When he reached the age of maturity in 1553 George Barley sued Freschevile, Sir William Cavendish, Bess, and Edward Bowne, an attorney in the Common Bench, for spoil of his estates. TNA, C 1/1291/17 (dateable to

the first half of 1553). Among the replies of the defendants is one made by Sir William and Bess which states that Robert was *already* seised of his estates when he married Bess, TNA, C 1/1291/18. This implies that Robert's marriage to Bess may have actually taken place shortly after Arthur Barley's death. If this was the case, then Freschevile may not have been exaggerating when he claimed that Robert had been abducted but it is more likely that Freschevile was attempting to convince the court that Robert had been forced to marry Bess and was, therefore, married under duress. Freschevile did not say, and indeed may not have known exactly when Bess's marriage had taken place but his proceedings clearly implied it could have been shortly after, if not shortly before, Arthur Barley's death.

[12] Riden,'The Hardwicks', 152. TNA, C 1/1291/17-21. From the early fourteenth century the Barley's are recorded as holding lands and tenements in Barley partly by half a knight's service of the Freschevile's manor of Staveley. *Collectanea, 183.* Arthur Barley's IPM states that the manor of Barley was ' held of Peter Frechewell, esquire, as of two parts of his manor of Staveley, by service of half a knight's fee and suit of court, and worth £13 6s 8d p.a', TNA, WARD 7/1/66 (no.164), E 150/753/2 and C 142/68/51. George Barley continued to seek redress and in 1559, following the death of Freschevile in 1558, he petitioned Lord Keeper Bacon stating in his submission that 'After Robert died, Sir Peter Frechevyle, now deceased, a man then of great power, without right entered the lands, claiming to be George's guardian, supposing the lands to be held of him by knight service, when in fact they are held by socage tenure and not by knight service'. George claimed he had no remedy at common law against the administrator for the deeds of Sir Peter, and thus asked for a writ of subpoena to Sir Peter's heir, Peter Freschevile, esquire, ordering him to appear in Chancery, to answer the charges and abide by the court's decision. TNA, C 3/11/108.

[13] Riden,'The Hardwicks', n. 72, 169, citing TNA, C 1/860/14-15. This was also the period during which Ralph was facing imprisonment in the Fleet and accusations of desertion by his wife.

[14] TNA, C1/1101/17; T. Kilburn, 'Wardship and Marriage', 199; P. Riden, 'The Hardwicks of Hardwick Hall in the Fifteenth and Sixteenth Centuries', Derbyshire Archaeological Journal, 130 (2010), 151. See also Chapter 5.

[15] A. Flower, *Tudor Women's Legal Rights, 1485-1603*, (2007), 25

[16] G. D. Barlow, *Published Matter and Records relating to the Families of the Name Barlow* (1911), contains a printed pedigree based on the visitations of 1569 and 1611 inserted after page 20. Sir Montague Barlow, *Barlow Family Records* (1932). Pedigree number 5, inserted between pages 16 - 17. The Belvoir Castle manuscript pedigree, see n.9 above, includes the marriage of George Barley to Jane Freschevile.

[17] The case against Ralph was brought by a Robert Stokes, TNA: STAC 2/28/49; Riden., 'The Hardwicks', 157; Wykes v Waterhowse, TNA: STAC: 20/2/40, fol 1r.

[18] Riden, *ibid*, 151-2

[19] In 1543 Robert's mother, Elizabeth Barley, Arthur Barley's widow, began a Common Pleas action in for dower, Hilary Term, 1544, against Robert Barley, Peter Freschevile esq, Ralph Leche and Henry Marmion. TNA, CP 40/1120 (AALT IMG 5387). Her case was contemporaneous with Freschevile's proceedings against Ralph Leche, Bess's mother and Marmion. Although her son Robert was still a minor, she was unable to identify his guardian, presumably because the court was yet to determine Freschevile's case. see appendix 2a. Her claim for dower was accepted unchallenged by Freschevile, Easter Term, 1545. TNA, CP 40/1125 (AALT IMG 0262), see appendix 2b; Bess's cousin, Catherine Leake, married Sir Godfrey Foljambe. Their son, Sir George, married Robert's sister, Dorothy. The Foljambes were also suing Freschevile for Dorothy's unpaid marriage portion.

[20] TNA, C 1/1101/17, appendix 5, is Bess's initial complaint to Chancery presented to Sir Thomas Wriothesley who became Lord Chancellor on the 3rd of May 1544. Bess informed Chancery that she had been a widow for eighteen months which indicates that she began her Chancery action in mid-1546. The final section of the document is badly damaged with many words missing but provides details of Bess's attempts to obtain dower including references to her 1545 Common Pleas proceedings and to events that had taken place earlier in 1546. Bess also refers to having been "married and

espoused" to Robert but later reverses the order to "espoused and married". Wright, *Derbyshire Gentry*, 122, argues it was common practice among the gentry of north-east Derbyshire to engage an arbiter in an effort to resolve disputes even when court proceedings were already in progress. The Chaworths were related to the Frescheviles, the Leakes, the Hardwicks and the Barleys, and had acted as feofees of certain Hardwick and Barley lands. TNA, WARD 7/1/66 (no.164).

[21] TNA, C 1/1101/17 states that Arthur Barley was paid by the '[...]' of Elizabeth. Unfortunately, the word here is faded and virtually illegible, even under UV light, although it is almost certainly one word and given the context in which it occurs is most likely the word 'friends' by which Bess may have meant Ralph Leche and Henry Marmion and possibly Godfrey Boswell.

[22] For a detailed discussion of Ralph's finances see Riden, 'The Hardwicks', 153-5.

[23] TNA, CP 40/1092 (AALT IMG 2706); TNA, CP 40/1096 (AALT IMG 2393)

[24] Riden, 'The Hardwicks', 155. As husband and wife were considered to be a 'single soul', Bess's mother could not sue Ralph under Common Law but she could do so in a court of equity. TNA, C1 845/34, see appendix 5. Flower, *Legal Rights*, 15. Frechevile's proceedings suggests that Ralph and Elizabeth were reconciled no later than 1543.

[25] TNA, STAC 2/19/310 Ralph's plea for debt against Arthur Barley and Ralph Aleyn's case against Leche. The Poultry Compter, in the parish of St Mildred, Cheap ward, was one of several debtors prisons under the control of the city of London sheriffs.

[26] Riden, 'The Hardwicks', 153-4

[27] TNA, C 1/1101/17.

APPENDIX 1 – Peter Freschevile's allegations of the abduction and illegal marriage of Robert Barley, TNA, CP 40/1120 (AALT IMG 7469). Crown copyright.

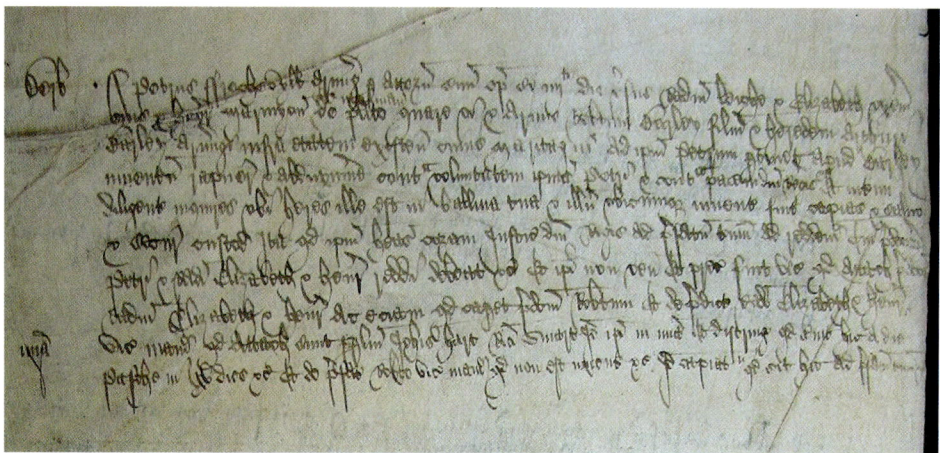

Derbyshire

Peter Frechevyll Esquire by his attorney brought a case on the fourth day against Ralph Leiche and Elizabeth his wife and Henry Marmyon \of …man/ concerning a plea why with force and arms they did take and abduct Robert Barley, having been found at Barley, the son and heir of Arthur Barley Esquire, being under age, whose marriage belongs to this Peter, against the will of this Peter and against the peace of the Lord the King, And meanwhile you shall diligently enquire where he the heir is in your bailiwick, and wheresoever you shall find him you shall take him and keep him safely and securely so that you shall have him before the Justices of the Lord the King at the said term to return unto whom of the said Peter and Ralph Elizabeth and Henry he ought to return etc. And they did not come. And the Sheriff was ordered to attach Ralph Elizabeth and Henry and also that he should seize the said Robert. And concerning the said Ralph Elizabeth and Henry the Sheriff orders that they are attached by the pledge of John

Hart and Richard Smart. Therefore they are in mercy. And distrain them so that they be here on the Quindene of Easter etc. And concerning the said Robert the Sheriff orders that he is not found etc, so he should be seized so that he be here at the said term.

APPENDIX 2a - Elizabeth Barley, widow of Arthur Barley, Common Pleas proceedings for dower, 1543/4. TNA, CP 40/1120 (AALT IMG 5387). Crown copyright.

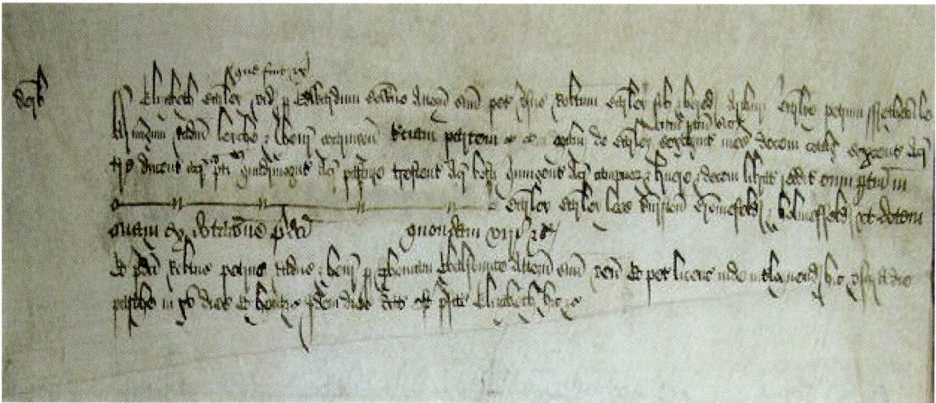

Derbyshire

Elizabeth Barley widow (who was the wife), by Edward Bowne her attorney, demands against Robert Barley son [interlined] and heir of Arthur Barlye, Peter Frechevile Esquire, Ralph Leyche and Henry Marmyon, one third part [written over erasure "her....."] of the manor of Barley with appurtenances and 60 messuages, 10 cottages, 600 acres of land, 200 acres of meadow, 40 acres of pasture, 300 acres of woodland, 50 acres of furze and heath and £10 of rent with appurtenances in [long erasure] Barley, Barley Lees, Dronefeld and Holmesfeld as her dower by the endowment of the said [blank] formerly her husband etc. And the said Robert, Peter, Ralph and Henry, by Thomas Chalfounte their attorney, come and here seek licence to imparl until the quindene of Easter. And they have [it] etc. The same day is here given to the said Elizabeth etc.

APPENDIX 2b - Elizabeth Barley, widow of Arthur Barley, Common Pleas proceedings for dower, Hilary Term. 1545. TNA, CP 40/1125 (AALT IMG 0262). Crown copyright.

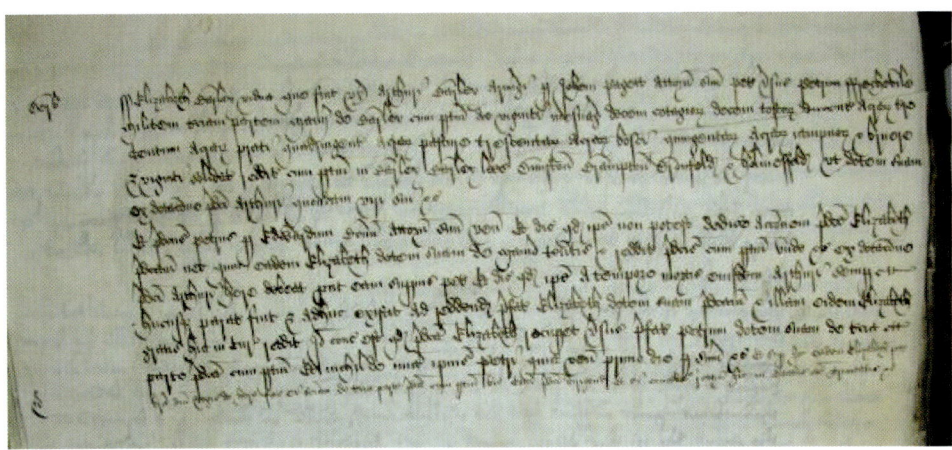

Derbyshire

Elizabeth Barley widow, who was the wife of Arthur Barley, Esquire, represented by John Pagett her attorney, demands against Peter Frechevile, knight, one third part of the manor of Barley with appurtenances, and of twenty messuages, ten cottages, ten tofts, two hundred acres of arable land, one hundred acres of meadow, four hundred acres of pasture, three hundred acres of wood, five hundred acres of furze and heath, and twenty shillings rent, with appurtenances in Barley, Barley Lees, Dunston, Brampton, Dronfeld and Holmesfeld, as her dower by the endowment of the said Arthur formerly her husband, etcetera.

And the said Peter, represented by Edward Boun his attorney comes and says that he cannot oppose the said action of the said Elizabeth and that the same Elizabeth ought to have her dower of the manor, tenements and rents aforesaid with appurtenances, whereof etcetera, by the endowment of the said Arthur, just as she seeks above. And he says that he, since the time of the death of the same Arthur, always until now, has been prepared and still is prepared to render to the said Elizabeth her said dower and he freely renders it to the same Elizabeth here in court. So it is ordered that the said Elizabeth should recover against the said Peter her dower of one third part aforesaid with appurtenances, and nothing for penalty from him Peter because he came on the first day when summonsed etcetera. And hereupon the same Elizabeth seeks that a writ of the Lord the King be directed to the Sheriff of the said County concerning receiving possession unto her of the said third part with appurtenances, and it is granted to her, to be returned here in the Octave of Holy Trinity, etcetera.

APPENDIX 3 - Godfrey Boswell's purchase of Robert Barley's wardship, 1544. TNA, WARD 9/152. Crown copyright.

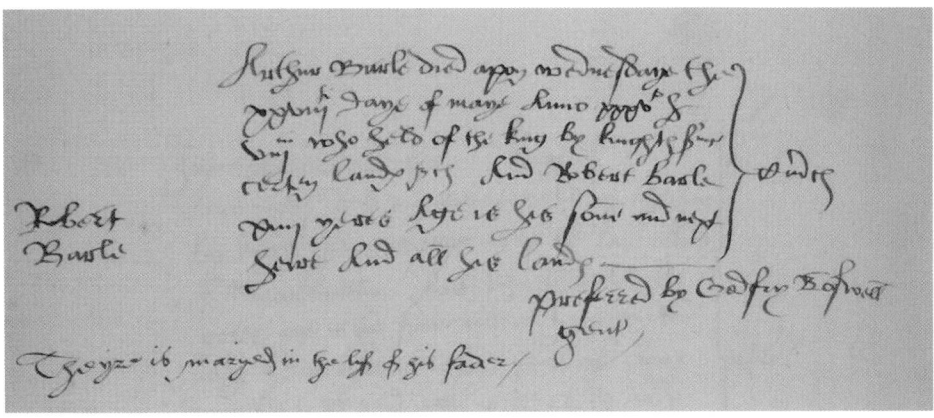

Robert marks Barle	Arthur Barle died upon Wednesday the 28th day of May year 35 Henry VIII, who held of the king by knight service certain lands etc. And Robert Barle 14 years age is his son and next heir and all his lands	100

                        Preferred by Godfry Boswell
                        gent

The heir is married in the life of his father

APPENDIX 4 - Elizabeth Leche v Ralph Leche. Chancery proceedings for desertion. TNA, C1 845/34. Crown copyright.

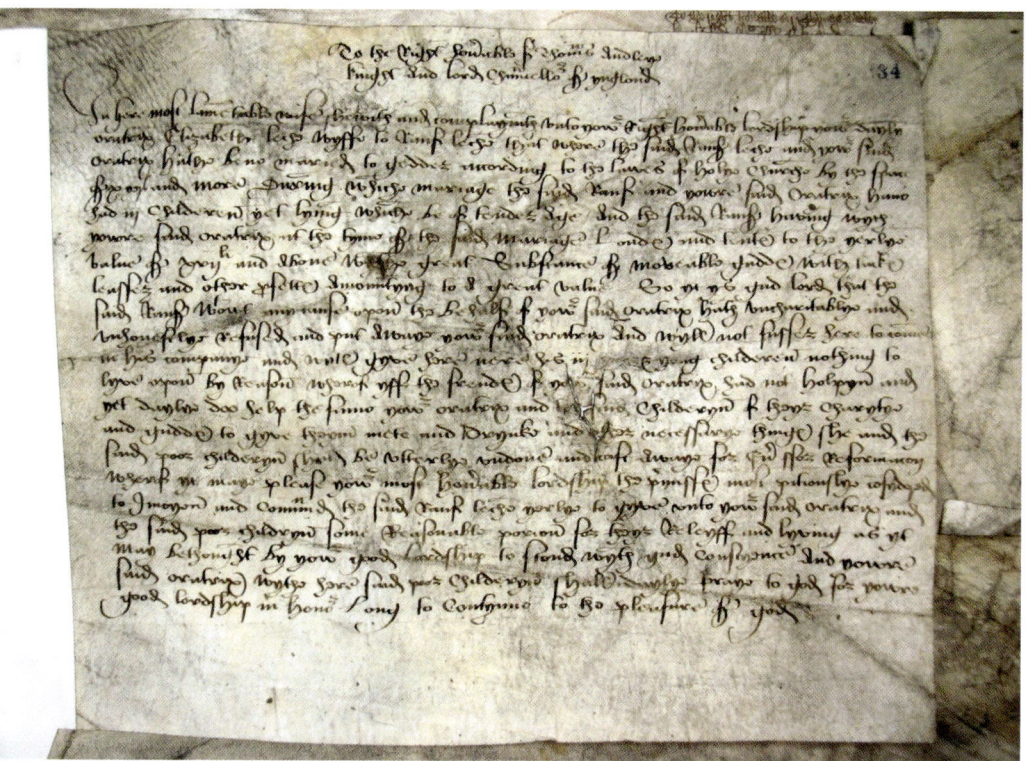

To the right honourable Sir Thomas Audley
knight and lord chancellor of England.[1]

In here most lamentable wise showeth and complaineth unto your right honourable lordship your daily oratrix Elizabeth Leche, wife to Rauf Leche, that where the said Rauf Leche and your said oratrix hath been married together according to the laws of holy church by the space of 10 years and more, during which marriage the said Rauf and your said oratrix have had 3 children yet living, which be of tender age, and the said Rauf, having with your said oratrix at the time of the said marriage lands and tenements to the yearly value of £17 and above, with great substance of moveable goods and with 'tacks',[2] leases and other profits amounting to a great value. So it is good lord that the said Rauf, without any cause upon the behalf of your said oratrix, hath uncharitably and unhonestly refused and put away your said oratrix, and will not suffer her to come in his company, and will give her nor his 3 poor[3] and young children nothing to live upon, by reason whereof, if the friends of your said oratrix had not helpen and yet daily do help the same your oratrix and her said children of their charity and goods, to give them meat and drink and other necessary things, she and the said poor children should be utterly undone and cast away for ever. For reformation whereof it may please your most honourable lordship, the premises most piteously considered, to enjoin and command the said Rauf Leche yearly to give unto your said oratrix and the said poor children some reasonable portion for their relief and living as it may be thought by your good lordship to stand with good conscience. And your said oratrix with her said poor children shall daily pray to God for your good lordship, in honour long to continue, to the pleasure of God.

---

[1] After his elevation in 1538 Audley would have been addressed as Lord or Baron and not as 'Sir'. All three of Elizabeth's children fathered by Ralph were born by 1534. This document must then date from between 1534 and 1538.

[2] This word appears to read 'tacks' or 'tackes', but the third letter is unclear. The word 'tack' could refer to a type of lease, but was primarily a Scottish term[?] It may perhaps just refer to money being 'taken', i.e. in the form of rents, etc. It could also be 'taxes' but unlikely.

[3] This word has been written over an erasure; it is badly faded but under UV light appears to read 'poor'.

APPENDIX 5 - Transcript of, Bess of Hardwick's complaint to Chancery, Trinity Term, (20 June – mid- July), 1546. TNA, C 1/1101/17. Crown copyright.

To the right honourable Sir Thomas Wryothesley, knight

of the honourable order of the garter, Lord

Wryothesley and Lord Chancellor of England.

In most humble wise complaining showeth unto your honourable lordship your daily oratrice Elizabeth Barley, widow, late the wife of Robert Barley, esquire, deceased, son and heir of//

Arthur Barley, esquire, also deceased, that whereas the said Arthur Barley was lawfully seised of and in the manor of Barley with appurtenances in the county of Derby, and of [...]//

messuages, ten cottages, one thousand acres of land, three hundred acres of meadow, six hundred acres of pasture, four hundred acres of wood, six hundred acres of furze and heath, and//

ten pounds of rent with their appurtenances in Barlow, Barlow Lees, Dunston, Dronfield and Holmesfield in the said county of Derby, in his demesne as of fee, all which manor, lands, tenements and//

premises being of the yearly value of £80 and above, and the said Arthur Barley, so being seised of the said manor, lands, tenements and premises, did covenant and bargain with the friends//

of your said oratrice for a marriage to be had between the said Robert and your said oratrice, in consideration of diverse great sums of money paid by the friends of the same your//

oratrice to the said Arthur for the same, in the performance of which said bargain the said Robert Barley was lawfully married and espoused unto your said oratrice, the same Robert and//

your said oratrice being then but of tender years. And after, the said Arthur, so as is aforesaid being seised of the said manors, lands, tenements and premises in his demesne as of fee [...]//

such estate thereof seised in the 35th year [22 April 1543 – 22 April 1544] of the reign of our sovereign lord the king that now is, the said Robert being then of the age of 13 years, after whose decease the said manor,//

lands, tenements and premises descended unto the said Robert Barley, as son and heir of the said Arthur, by force whereof the same Robert was lawfully seised of and in the said manor,//

lands, tenements and all other the premises in his demesne as of fee. And the said Robert, so being seised of the premises, about the last day of December in the ?36th year [22 April 1544 – 22 April 1545] of the//

reign of our sovereign lord the king that now is [Henry VIII] of such estate thereof died seised without any issue of his body lawfully begotten, after whose decease the said manor, lands, [...]//

premises being descended unto George Barley, esquire, as brother and heir of the said Robert, the same George being within the age of 21 years, by reason whereof Sir Peter//

Frechevyle, knight, supposing the said manor of Barley, parcel of the premises, to be holden of him by knight service, hath entered into the same manor of Barley [with appurtenances?]//

and hath the custody of the body of the same George and the residue of all the said lands, tenements and premises being in the hands of the said George, by reason that [...] are//

holden in socage, and that the same George is of the age of 14 years and [...] after the decease of which said Robert Barley for that your said oratrice is by the [...]//

usual laws of this realm lawfully entitled to be endowed of the third part of the said manor, lands, tenements and all other the premises she demanded and [...]//

the said Sir Peter as the said George to assign unto her the said dower thereof, which they unjustly and against all laws and equity refused to do, whereupon [...]//

oratrice was compelled to sue against the said Sir Peter and George Barley two several writs of dower returnable before the justices of our sovereign lord the [...]//

his common place at Westminster, to be endowed of the third part of premises, in the which said writs, after the same had long depended before the said [...]//

any answer made unto the same, to the great cost and charge and delay of your said poor oratrice, the said Sir Peter and the said George by the procurement [?of the]//

same Sir Peter, untruly pleaded that the said Robert Barley, during the espousal and marriage between him and your said oratrice, was never seised [...]//

estate whereof she ought to be endowed, which said plea is untrue and only pleaded to the intent to delay and fatigue your said poor oratrice, being [...]//

friends, aid or comfort and not able to try the said issue untruly tendered by the said Sir Peter and George by the order of the common laws [...]//

thereby to accept a final recompense for her said lawful dower at the pleasure of the said Sir Peter and George, for since the said untrue plea pleaded [...]//

to say in the term of Saint Hilary [20 Jan – to mid-February] - in the 37th year [April 1545 – April 1546] of the reign of our said sovereign lord, Sir John Chaworth, knight, uncle to the said George, by his [...]//

and assent of the said Sir Peter as of the said George, knowing right well that your said oratrice ought to be endowed of the premises and diverse [...]//

proffer unto the council of your said oratrice that if she would be contented to demise and let to farm all her said third part of the premises [...]//

friends for a certain yearly rent to be reserved for the same, that then they would waive and relinquish the said untrue plea and issue and [...]//

poor oratrice, which thing your said oratrice, being enforced thereunto by necessity, by the advice of her council, was contented to do, and [...]//

the said Sir John Chaworth and the council of your said oratrice, the same Sir John Chaworth would not assent that there should [...]//

upon the said demised and fortreated lease of the said third part, but only £16, where of truth the just third part of the same [...]//

£26 13s 4d, which notwithstanding your said oratrice rather constrained by necessity than compelled by equity, was contented to accept [...]//

her dower, which the said Sir John Chaworth also refused, by reason whereof the said untrue plea remaining now to be tried [...]//

the king's justices of nisi prius, wherein the said Sir Peter and George are inhabiting, and your said poor oratrice without any friends [...]//

her to her trial of her said just title. And so, right honourable lord, for as much as Ralph Leeche, who hath married the mother of your said [...]//

condemned in great sums of money and her said mother very poor and not able to relieve herself and much less your said oratrice, and for [...]//

not nor had any substance or other advancement but only the said title of dower by her said late husband who died, being very ly[...]//

not of ability to proceed to the trial of the said issues and untrue pleas against the said Sir Peter and George by the order of the common law [...]//

for the same, suffering the said most apparent wrong and injuries, living as she hath done by the space of one year and a half since the [...]//

succour or comfort of the said lands. In tender consideration whereof it may please your good lordship to grant the king's gracious w[rit?] [...]//

Sir Peter and George straightly enjoining and commanding them by the same upon a certain pain by your good lordship[...]//

oratrice her lawful third part of the said manor, lands, tenements and premises, and to pay unto her all the arrears [...]//

the decease of her said late husband, or else to permit and suffer the same your oratrice to have, occupy and enjoy the third part [...]//

premises and the rents and revenues of the same third part, to have and take to her own proper use, without any impediment [...]//

Frechevyle and George or any of them, or of any person or persons by their commandment, procurement or consent, or to their use [...]//

otherwise licensed by your good lordship, and your said poor oratrice shall daily pray to God for the good estate of your good lor[dship] [...]//

2

Sir William Cavendish, Marriage to Bess and Relocation to Derbyshire

Four times the nuptial bed she warm'd,
And every time so well perform'd,
That when death spoil'd each husband's billing,
He left the widow every shilling ...

Walpole.

Horace Walpole was not impressed with Hardwick Hall. It was not to his taste. Having been told he would be utterly charmed by the house, he wrote 'never was I less charmed in my life'. Referring to Bess as 'that old beldam', he determined to write her an 'epitaph'.[1]

Walpole was not the first, nor would he be the last, to portray Bess as consummate schemer. In 1672 Sir William Dugdale wrote that Bess 'became Mistriss of a very vast fortune, by her successful matching with several wealthy Husbands'.[2] In 1838 Edmund Lodge stated that Bess, 'unsated with the wealth and the caresses of three husbands finished her conquests by marrying the earl of Shrewsbury, the richest and most powerful peer of his time.'[3] These authors failed to recognise that Bess had to struggle through both common law and equity courts to secure dower from her marriage to Robert Barley[4] and she was said to be penniless when Sir William Cavendish died in 1557.[5]

Despite two previous marriages Cavendish was still in need of a male heir at the time of his marriage to Bess. Shortly after the marriage he commenced his move to Derbyshire. Philip Riden has noted that both Sir William's marriage to Bess and his subsequent decision to relocate lock, stock and barrel to Derbyshire have 'never been satisfactorily explained'.[6] The first to claim that Sir William's move to Chatsworth came at the 'desire' of Bess was Arthur Collins in 1752, though without explaining what that desire was.[7]

It has been suggested that the only reason to accept Collins's statement is that 'it is difficult to think of any other reason why an official at court would give up an estate conveniently close to London ... and move to a much more remote county ...'.[8] Cavendish was not alone among his rank and calling to seek to create a land-based posterity but was the choice of Derbyshire merely to satisfy the whim of his new wife, as some have supposed? Concern for her safety may have played a more important role than caprice. Sir William saw his principal estate at Northaw, Hertfordshire, become the target of anti-enclosure riots in May 1548. Local protests over Cavendish's use of common land erupted in 1544 when he attempted to enclose some 500 acres of Northaw Great Waste.[9] He was alleged to have over-stocked the commons with rabbits and sheep. The 1548 riots were a continuation of this dispute, a reaction to a royal commission granted to Sir William in the king's name by the newly appointed Lord Protector, Edward Seymour. Cavendish claimed that on the 21 May around sixty rioters camped outside his house and laid siege to the property. Sir William, a heavily pregnant Bess, other members of his family and visitors to the property were trapped inside.

Cavendish alleged that numerous attempts were made to break into the house and that the rioters threatened to burn down the property and all those within if he did not come out and face them. They inflicted considerable damage at Northaw, including the use of explosives to destroy Sir William's rabbit warrens along with around 1,000 rabbits on Northaw Common. A second attack on the warrens took place the following day resulting in the deaths of a further 300 rabbits which were slaughtered 'amidst a volley of bone-chilling cries.' Cavendish alleged that his chaplain and some of his servants were attacked during the rioting. On the nights of the 25th and 26th Sir William claimed to have been awakened by 'hallowing, cryeng and yelling' coming from outside his house, frightening his wife and family, as the rioters continued to hunt in the nearby warrens, and that during the first night the rioters stole a trotting horse and five geldings from his stables.[10] These events must have been - at the very least - unsettling for Bess. We cannot rule out the possibility that they contributed to Sir William's decision to leave Northaw but does this alone fully explain why he moved to Derbyshire? The anti-enclosure disturbances were suppressed during the late summer and early autumn of 1549. The purchase of Chatsworth and Cromford did not take place until December 1549, some eighteen months after the 1548 riots at Northaw and Cavendish's move to Derbyshire was not completed until 1552.[11] The rioting at Northaw in 1544 simmered on until 1548. It reflected local grievances borne by the tenants against the activities of a relative newcomer but also presaged the more widespread and better-known anti-enclosure rioting of 1549. It has been suggested that Sir William 'may have been driven out of Hertfordshire by local animosity.'[12] He was still described as being of Northaw, Chatsworth and London in 1553.[13] The anti-enclosure disturbances did, however, play a significant role in the demise of Protector Somerset, a point to which we will return.

In seeking to explain both Sir William's marriage to Bess and his relocation to Derbyshire historians may have been looking in the wrong place. Could Sir William's decisions have been influenced far more by events at the centre of government during and after Edward VI's reign than has been recognised? Can it be mere chance that his move to Derbyshire coincided with Edward Seymour's fall from power and the later attempt to place Lady Jane Grey on the throne? Are there too many such coincidences for them to be ignored? Those familiar with the high politics of the mid-sixteenth century, a period often referred to as the mid-Tudor crisis,[14] will recognise the difficulties in acquiring a full understanding of affairs at court, the epicentre of political life during this tumultuous period. The politics of the period remain steeped in obfuscation as over the intervening centuries untruths have been told and documents distorted, destroyed or otherwise 'lost', whilst many of those involved sought to cover up their roles in the dramas that afflicted the realm at this critical juncture in English history. The easiest way to find someone guilty was to use their own words against them and a search of an accused person's private papers would be among the first stages of any investigation. Those accused would look to destroy such evidence before it could be found. As John Flower put it to Thomas Seymour in 1548, once gone such evidence 'shall tell no more tales.'[15] Shortly before his arrest in October 1549 Thomas's brother, Edward Seymour, Lord Protector, gave orders that his papers should be destroyed[16] and following his abortive revolt in 1601 the earl of Essex busied himself setting fire to his papers.[17] There are many similar examples.

Bess's first marriage to Robert Barley lasted less than two years. The notion that Bess became a wealthy woman on Robert's death is false. The family estate was inherited, not by Bess, but by Robert's younger brother, George, the ward of Peter Freschevile who challenged the legality of Bess's marriage to Robert and refused to pay her dower.[18] As indicated in her later complaint to the Court of Chancery, early in 1545 Bess commenced proceedings for dower in the Court of Common Pleas.[19] In mid-1546, seeking a swifter resolution, she turned to Chancery. She stated that two writs had been issued on her behalf against Freschevile but that he had deliberately prevaricated in order to 'delay and fatigue' her Common Pleas proceedings which she could no longer afford to continue. She was willing to settle the dispute for 40 marks (£26 13s. 4d.),[20] hardly a sum on which to commence building a dynasty.

Quoting from Sir William Cavendish's pocketbook Arthur Collins informs us that the marriage of Sir William and Bess took place at 2 a.m. on 20 August 1547 at Bradgate Park, the Leicestershire home of Henry Grey, marquis of Dorset.[21] Grey's wife, Frances, was the daughter of Charles Brandon and his wife Mary, dowager queen of France, Henry VIII's sister. Frances was therefore the cousin of Henry VIII's daughters, Mary and Elizabeth, and his son, Edward. In 1551, following the death from sweating sickness of the two sons of his father-in-law, Grey became duke of Suffolk. By 1545 Henry and Frances Grey had three daughters under five. Only six months older than Prince Edward, Lady Jane Grey was born in October 1537, her parents then being just 20 and 21 years of age. 1540 saw the birth of Jane's sister, Katherine, and the youngest of the Grey sisters, Mary, was born in 1545. That same year Bess commenced her Barley dower proceedings. Sir William's marriage to Bess took place at the Grey's principal county seat but little is known about this period of Bess's life. Henry and Frances and their daughters Jane and Katherine stood as godparents to one or more of Sir William and Bess's children. Henry was godfather to their sons, Henry and Charles. Their first child, Frances, was christened in honour of her godmother, Frances Grey. Their first son, Henry, was almost certainly named for Henry Grey and Charles may have been named for Charles Brandon. Along with her mother, Jane Grey stood as godmother to Sir William and Bess's second daughter, Temperance, and Katherine Grey was godmother to their daughter Elizabeth.[22] Bess was of a similar age to Frances Grey. A portrait of 'my lady Jane' listed at Chatsworth in the 1560s is believed to have been kept by Bess on her bedside table.[23] It has even been improbably claimed that Jane and

Katherine Grey were bridesmaids at Bess's marriage to Sir William.[24] However, there is no evidence to substantiate the claim that following the death of Robert Barley Bess entered the service of the Greys.[25]

Here again, historians may have been looking in the wrong place. Henry Marmion, gent, crops up at various stages in the story of the Hardwicks. Together with John Leake, he was an executor of John Hardwick's will and remained close to the Hardwicks after John's death in 1528. John's son and heir, James, was around three years of age when his father died and thus subject to wardship. In March 1530 James's wardship was sold by the Court of Wards for £20 to a courtier named John Bugby. Probably with a degree of conventional exaggeration, in 1533 Bugby claimed he had been forcibly evicted from Hardwick Hall by a gang of men led by John Leake and Marmion.[26] Around 1540 Marmion appears to have masterminded an alleged attack at Chatsworth for which he, Bess's mother and others, were brought before the Derby assizes and later investigated by Star Chamber.[27]

Henry Marmion was a servant of the Willoughbys of Wollaton. There were long standing connections between the Hardwicks and the Willoughbys.[28] Sir Henry Willoughby married Anne Grey, the sister of Henry Grey of Bradgate. Sir Henry and Anne had a daughter, Margaret, and two sons, Thomas and Francis. Anne died in 1548 and following their father's death in 1549 the two boys were subject to wardship. Francis, aged three, became the ward of his maternal uncle, Henry Grey. On Thomas's death in 1559 the Willoughby estates passed to Francis who as Sir Francis Willoughby was to become the builder of Wollaton Hall. It is quite possible that Bess's long association with Sir Francis Willoughby may have begun at Bradgate. Bess was twenty-three years old when she became a widow for the first time. The bequests made to Bess in her father's will were spent and given his own financial difficulties it is likely that Ralph Leche did not wish to incur the costs of her return to the family home. It is possible to speculate that perhaps at the intercession of Henry Marmion Bess may have been in service to the Willoughbys rather than the Greys. The Willoughbys were regular visitors to Bradgate.

William Cavendish's career as a bureaucrat began in the 1520s. Possibly on the recommendation of his brother George, around 1530 he entered the service of Thomas Cromwell.[29] William's entry into Cromwell's service coincided with Wolsey's fall and the beginning of his new master's meteoric rise to power during the 1530s. It was likely to Cromwell that Sir William owed his introductions to both the Greys and the Seymours. Cavendish owned a picture of 'Lord Cromwell' and among the portraits in the Long Gallery at Hardwick Hall is a rare painting of Edward Seymour. This portrait was probably among those known to have been owned by Sir William at his home at Northaw.[30] Edward Seymour was the elder brother of Henry VIII's third wife, Jane Seymour, mother of Prince Edward. Along with Edward Seymour, Cromwell encouraged Henry VIII's courtship and marriage to Jane. Cromwell's son, Gregory, became the second husband of Queen Jane's sister, Elizabeth Seymour. It was probably as a servant of Cromwell that Cavendish came to the attention of Edward Seymour, who in 1536 appointed William to the post of auditor of the newly created Court of Augmentations. William spent much of following three years in the Home Counties and the Midlands receiving the surrender of religious houses.[31] During this time he must have developed a wide network of associates and contacts. Cavendish was knighted in 1546 and sat as MP for Thirsk in the 1547 parliament. The seat was in the gift of either Cromwell's former protégé Robert Holgate, archbishop of York and President of the Council of the North, or the borough's lord, Edward Stanley, 3rd earl of Derby. Despite his later apostasy, at this time Holgate was a supporter of evangelical reform, whereas Stanley was rightly suspected of being Catholic. It may have been Edward Seymour who recommended Cavendish to Holgate.[32] Sir William was also an associate of Seymour's steward, Sir John Thynne of Longleat, at one point seeking Sir John's help to find a plasterer for Chatsworth,[33] a request Bess repeated in 1560.[34] In 1553 Thynne became comptroller of Princess Elizabeth's household. Sir William was an associate of the Greys who, in turn, were closely allied to Seymour, to Catherine Parr's brother William, and to John Dudley. At the time of his marriage to Bess, Cavendish was renting his London house in Aldersgate from Parr.[35] Sir William's first wife, Margaret Bostock, died in 1540. Although the marriage produced two surviving daughters, Cavendish lacked a male heir. Perhaps he cast an eye over Bess at Bradgate yet it is also possible that his eye may have been pointed in Bess's direction by the Greys.

Following Henry VIII's death in January 1547 Edward Seymour used his position as the boy-king's uncle to establish himself as Lord Protector of

England and Governor of the King's Person. By the end of March 1547, he had also taken for himself the title of duke of Somerset, a title with royal connotations having been held previously by Henry VIII's Beaufort ancestors and by the late king's illegitimate son, Henry Fitz-Roy. There were particularly close connections between the Greys and the Seymours. Henry Grey and Edward Seymour had known each other from boyhood and, along with William Parr, served in Fitz-Roy's household.[36] In February 1549 Grey and Seymour discussed a possible marriage between Lady Jane Grey, third in line to the throne, and Seymour's son Edward, earl of Hertford.[37] Frances Grey's mother died in June 1533 and three months later her father, Charles Brandon, married his ward, the 14-year-old Katherine Willoughby, and took control of her family's extensive properties in Lincolnshire and elsewhere.[38] Katherine would later become the patron and protector of bible translator Myles Coverdale.

In the early months of 1547 Edward Seymour's younger brother, Thomas, 1st Lord Sudeley, married Henry VIII's widow, Catherine Parr. Thomas resented his elder brother's influence over their nephew, Edward VI, and envied the power that came with this influence. Although promoted to the rank of Lord High Admiral, he felt strongly that the offices of Lord Protector and Governor of the King's Person should not have been held by the same person. As the king's other uncle, he took the view that the latter position rightly belonged to him. Despite the opposition of Frances Grey and the unease of her husband, Thomas had persuaded Henry Grey to allow the ten-year-old Lady Jane Grey to join his household by promising to promote a marriage between Jane and the king.[39] Rumours spread that Thomas intended to marry Jane but his sights were set on a greater prize. Shortly before his marriage to Catherine, Thomas offered his hand in marriage to the king's sister, Princess Elizabeth.[40] Elizabeth declined his proposal but for a while was placed in the Admiral's household. His petting and other improper behaviour towards the princess so alarmed Catherine that she had Elizabeth moved elsewhere. Following Catherine's death Thomas was suspected of seeking to renew his suit with the princess.[41] Edward Seymour had been infuriated by his brother's marriage to Catherine and thereafter relations between the brothers deteriorated further. By early 1549 intense jealousy of his brother finally drove Thomas to seek to gain control of Edward VI. Arrested on suspicion of plotting to kidnap the king, he was found guilty of treason and executed in March 1549.[42] Things also went badly for Somerset. The Lord Protector consistently ignored William Paget's warnings that many members of the Privy Council resented his autocratic style of government.[43] By October 1549 Seymour was under arrest and the Protectorate was at an end. Among those placed in the Tower for being 'principal instruments and counsellors ... in the affairs of his ill government' was Sir John Thynne.[44] Seymour's position as Lord Protector had been ratified on the final day of the 1547 parliament. Two years later Edward VI noted in his journal that by another Act of Parliament, 'The Lord Protector lost, by his own agreement and submission, his protectorship, treasurership, marshalship, all his moveables and near £2,000 worth of land.'[45]

When Mary Tudor commenced her rebellion against Queen Jane in 1553 John Dudley, duke of Northumberland, and William Parr, marquis of Northampton, led the party sent to Norfolk to arrest her. As it became clear that the scheme to keep Jane on the throne was doomed many, including almost every member of the Privy Council, abandoned her cause and blamed the entire affair on Dudley. Cavendish certainly had affinity with those who sought to place Jane Grey on the throne and with the principals of the Wyatt rebellion. A portrait of Wyatt is listed in the Hardwick inventory of 1601.[46] Wyatt was yet another of Thomas Cromwell's protégés and Sir William is likely to have met him after entering Cromwell's service. Although there is no documentary evidence to show that Sir William was involved in the attempt to prevent Mary Tudor's succession or that he had any involvement in the Wyatt rebellion, his affinities, his circle and his position as a senior official suggest that he must at least have been aware of events. Changing sides in the interest of self-preservation was a powerful motivator in an age in which a likely alternative was losing one's head on the block. William Paulet, earl of Wiltshire, William Cecil, and Henry Grey, for example, had little hesitation switching allegiance from Somerset to Dudley,[47] and Sir John Thynne, among others, found no difficulty proclaiming Mary Tudor queen on the realisation that the Jane Grey episode was at an end.[48]

During the spring of 1551 Somerset was joined by the earls of Shrewsbury, Arundel and Derby in an alleged plot to overthrow Dudley. The main objective of the plot appears to have been the assassination of Dudley. A botched attempt on Dudley's life led to Arundel's arrest. Shrewsbury and

Derby looked to distance themselves from the whole affair.[49] Somerset's role in the conspiracy led to his trial and execution, although much of the evidence against him came from yet another turncoat, his former servant Sir Thomas Palmer, who was later to confess that much of the evidence he had given against Somerset had been fabricated.

Mary Tudor's successful revolt against Queen Jane resulted in pretty much the entire Privy Council abandoning John Dudley to his fate.[50] Cavendish was to claim he that had spent 1,000 marks raising men on Mary's behalf.[51] Though there is no evidence to the contrary, his Protestant leanings, close association with the Greys and members of their affinity make this seem dubious. Sir William's career was far more likely to have prospered had Jane remained on the throne rather than - as events were to prove – with Mary as queen. Lady Jane and Guildford Dudley were executed on the 12 February 1554 and her father's head placed on the execution block eleven days later. Wyatt's execution followed on 11 April. However, it was neither feasible nor indeed practical for Mary to dispose of her entire civil service in this way. It was probably Dudley who had blocked Cavendish's bid to become sheriff of Nottinghamshire and Derbyshire in November 1552 and it was possibly because he was not known to have been a close associate of Dudley that Sir William was among those who successfully sued for a general pardon and managed to survive in the aftermath of the Jane Grey affair.[52] Unlike several other senior officials,[53] he retained his office of Treasurer of the Chamber but in a diminished capacity receiving far fewer Privy Council warrants under Mary, suggesting that he was never fully trusted by the new Queen. It has been said that during his later years Sir William spent more time on domestic matters than professional ones.[54] In April 1557 an investigation was ordered into his accounts.[55] It was alleged that he owed the crown £5,237 5s. He admitted the debt and at the same time asked the Privy Council to show mercy to Bess and their children.[56] He died aged 49 in October 1557, Bess praying to the Lord 'to ridd mee and his poore Children of our greate Misserie'.[57] When a bill for the recovery of Sir William's debt was introduced into parliament one of the first people Bess turned to for help was her 'very good friend' Sir John Thynne.[58]

Historians have not examined sufficiently the question of how these momentous events may have influenced Sir William's decisions to marry Bess and relocate to Derbyshire. The early stirrings of the most serious rebellion of Henry VIII's reign, the 1536 Pilgrimage of Grace, began west of the Pennines in Lancashire but quickly spread into Yorkshire and Lincolnshire. In the aftermath of the rebellion the king sought to impose his authority in the north and ordered Charles Brandon to transfer the main centre of his operations from Suffolk to Lincolnshire. By the time of his death in 1545 Brandon had laid the foundations of a major aristocratic anti-Catholic affinity and his leadership role within it passed to his son-in-law Henry Grey the then marquis of Dorset. Composed predominantly of supporters of evangelical reform and the Edwardian Reformation, this affinity formed a substantial bloc of powerful anti-Catholic opposition in the region. Its members included the Greys (Leicestershire, Lincolnshire, Staffordshire), the Willoughbys (Nottinghamshire, Lincolnshire, Staffordshire, Warwickshire), William Parr, marquis of Northampton (Lord Lieutenant of Cambridgeshire, Northamptonshire, Bedfordshire, Huntingdonshire and Norfolk) and Francis, 5th earl of Shrewsbury (Yorkshire, Derbyshire, Nottinghamshire, Staffordshire). It was an affinity well represented among the godparents of Sir William and Bess's children. In addition to the Greys, these included numerous members of the Greys' Protestant circle. Katherine Brandon (neé Willoughby), dowager duchess of Suffolk, and her son the young Henry, duke of Suffolk, were two of the three godparents to Sir William's first child by Bess. The marchioness of Northampton, the 5th earl of Shrewsbury, the earl and countess of Warwick, the earl of Pembroke, and the Princess Elizabeth all became godparents to one or other of Sir William and Bess's children. Doubtless political expediency and pragmatism led to Mary Tudor and Stephen Gardiner joining Henry Grey as godparents to Sir William and Bess's fifth child, Charles, born early in Mary's reign. However, this did not deter the Cavendishes from reverting to their choice of Greys and Parrs as godparents to their sixth child, Elizabeth.[59]

Beneath the greater aristocratic affinities lay local connections. Intermarriage between neighbouring gentry families had made relatives of Leakes, Hardwicks, Leches, Boswells, Chaworths, Barleys, Markhams, Foljambes and Frescheviles. In an effort to make sense of contemporary political coteries, a manuscript book of pedigrees, probably drawn up at Haddon in the 1560s,[60] links families together in genealogical groupings. One of these groups is 'linea leeke gray et frechvyle'. Bess is included on account of her descent via her mother from the Leakes of Cotham and the Greys of Sandiacre. Other Derbyshire and Nottinghamshire families linked in this way include the Cartwrights, Watertons, Merings, Foljambes, Markhams, Tempests, Barleys and Cliftons. Among the Catholic families of Derbyshire were the Babingtons of Dethick, the FitzHerberts of Padley and the Eyres of Hassop. The Eyres supported Catholic enclaves at Hope, Dunston, Newbold and Hathersage. From the late fifteenth century much of Derbyshire no longer came under the control of any great magnate.[61] This meant that should there be any Catholic opposition to the reformation of religion during the reigns of Henry VIII and Edward VI north Derbyshire formed a potentially vulnerable area within an otherwise extensive central block of territory controlled by the Grey affinity. A potential weak link in the affinity was the conservative Francis, 5th earl of Shrewsbury who was known to be sympathetic to Catholicism and lukewarm towards reform. The 1536 Pilgrimage of Grace had in part spread through Talbot's main Yorkshire territories and coincided with the dissolution of the lesser monasteries in Derbyshire and elsewhere. In addition to Brandon's relocation to Lincolnshire, in October 1537 none other than the Lord Privy Seal, Thomas Cromwell, now armed with the powers of his recently acquired offices of Vice Gerent Over Spirituals and Vicar General, was added to the Derbyshire commission of the peace, 'his first known commission outside lowland England'.[62] The dissolution of Derbyshire's greater monasteries followed between 1538 and 1540.

Was Sir William Cavendish's marriage to Bess in 1547 part of an attempt by Henry Grey to plant a trustworthy ally in north Derbyshire? If so, was Bess merely a pawn in the hands of the Greys? Marriage to the daughter of a long-established north-east Derbyshire gentry family, the niece of another, the widow of a third, and whose brother-in-law and stepfather's family had recently been the owners of Chatsworth, would have ensured Sir William's ready acceptance in the county following his relocation to Derbyshire. Bess's mother, Elizabeth, was the daughter of Thomas Leake of Hasland, younger brother of Sir John Leake of Sutton. Bess was the widow of Robert Barley of Barlow Lees. By 1546 her sister, Jane, married Godfrey Boswell of Gunthwaite in south Yorkshire, whose four daughters all married into other Yorkshire gentry families. Another sister, Alice, married Francis Leche of Chatsworth who, in retaliation for his wife's infidelity, in 1547 rashly sold the estates of Chatsworth and Cromford to Thomas Agard. Like Cavendish,

Agard had been in Thomas Cromwell's service and was a client of Thomas Seymour. When Leche attempted to get back the properties he had sold, the Lord High Admiral gave his support to Agard. Leche went one better and appealed directly to Somerset who ordered that Agard could not deny the Leche family's right to inherit the properties. Thomas Agard died while this dispute was in progress and two years later his son, Francis Agard, brought the whole business to an end by selling the two manors to Sir William Cavendish and Bess.[63]

The timing of Sir William's marriage to Bess and his relocation to Derbyshire were indeed significant. Within weeks of the collapse of Somerset's Protectorate in the autumn of 1549, Sir William purchased the manors of Chatsworth and Cromford, after which he followed 'a policy of buying lands in Derbyshire on a considerable scale.'[64] Somerset was restored to the Privy Council on 10 April 1550, but he had failed to learn the lessons of 1549. He looked to regain his powers but in doing so quickly alarmed John Dudley and his supporters. Somerset was arrested on largely trumped-up charges, tried and found guilty.[65] Following in the footsteps of his younger brother, he was executed in January 1552. After the end of Somerset's Protectorate, John Dudley, earl of Warwick, took over the reins of government and the office of Grand Master of the King's Household, a role which incorporated the position of Lord President of the Council. Sir William Cavendish's parliamentary career ended in April 1552, with the close of the final session of the 1547 parliament, and just weeks after Somerset's execution Cavendish took the final steps in his move to Derbyshire. In June 1552, a mere six months after Somerset's death, Sir William sold Northaw and other holdings in southern England and a few in Wales to the Crown in exchange for mainly former monastic properties, including several in Derbyshire. His office still required his presence in the capital and he was therefore obliged retain a London residence, but he also began to hold local offices in Derbyshire.[66]

The 'planting' of Protestant families in the Midlands may have been aided by the distribution of former monastic lands. In 1546, during the minority of Henry, 2nd earl of Rutland, the Manners family surrendered their Northumberland estates in return for the Crown writing off their debt for the purchases of the Leicestershire priories of Belvoir and Croxton.[67] In 1547

Somerset exchanged various properties with the Crown for others nearer his estates in Somerset, Dorset and Oxfordshire, building up a substantial block of territory in the west of England.[68] Such exchanges, particularly of former monastic estates, not only helped to consolidate holdings but may also have been part of a centrally driven effort to systematically redraw the political map of England.

Edward VI died in July 1553, presumably in the knowledge that the terms of his 'devise for the succession'[69] would be implemented and that he would be succeeded by Jane Grey. Among many bequests, the king left £200 to Sir William.[70] Cavendish had been a good and loyal servant to both Edward and the king's uncle, the duke of Somerset. Furthermore, he was a member of the Grey affinity and a supporter of religious reform.[71] At the time of Edward VI's death, the establishment of Sir William Cavendish in north Derbyshire was well in hand. Although Henry Grey had been a close friend of Somerset, he recognised that he needed to be on good terms with the Lord President. Newly elevated as duke of Suffolk he distanced himself from the policies of the former Protector by playing a principal role in Somerset's trial and execution. Along with William Parr and William Herbert, now earl of Pembroke, Grey became closely associated with Dudley's government and was among the signatories of Edward VI's 'devise'. Early in 1553 Parr's wife, Elizabeth Brooke, appears to have brokered Jane Grey's marriage to Dudley's son, Guildford. In what became a triple wedding, Jane's sister Katherine married Henry Herbert, son of the earl of Pembroke, and Guildford's sister, another Katherine, married Francis Hastings, son of the earl of Huntingdon.[72]

Grey and Parr were the leading players in the attempt to place Jane on the throne.[73] Among those who were for Jane was Sir John St Loe.[74] He would have become Bess's father-in-law had he not died a few months before his son William married Bess in August 1559. Sir John was another member of the wider Grey affinity. The St Loes were also members of a West Country affinity which included the Seymours, Herberts, earls of Pembroke, the Courtenays, marquises of Exeter, the Bayntons and the Thynnes. Sir John St Loe was to become a thorn in the side of the Marian regime. He had held office under Henry VIII and in 1539 became a Groom of the Privy Chamber. Like Sir Edward Baynton, Sir John was a staunch evangelical Protestant. He was appointed a commissioner for the dissolution of chantries in Somerset. At the time of the Jane Grey affair, he was ordered by the Privy Council to muster forces in support of Jane. He had joined forces with Thynne at Longleat when Sir Nicholas Poyntz arrived with the news that Mary Tudor had been proclaimed queen in London. Thynne had no other option than to proclaim Mary Queen and did so at Warminster. St Loe rode to Somerset with like intent.[75] A letter arrived in Nottinghamshire from Bradgate ordering the assembled forces at Wollaton to be stood down.[76] Sir John St Loe remained active in local government but no longer attended court during Mary's reign. In 1556 a group of Protestant conspirators led by Sir Henry Dudley and Edward Courtney, marquis of Exeter, sought French help to drive Queen Mary into exile in Spain and place Princess Elizabeth on the throne. Suspected of being involved in the plot, Sir John's second son, Edward, was committed to the Fleet prison. Sir John was placed under house arrest at his London home. He died in March 1559.[77]

Sir John St Loe was the father of Bess's third husband, Sir William St Loe. By 1538 William was in the service of Edward Courtenay, second cousin to Edward VI. Courtenay was yet another principal of the Wyatt rebellion for which he spent a spell in the Tower before being released in 1555 due to a lack of evidence to convict him. Knighted under Seymour in 1549, following the death of Edward VI Sir William became a member of Princess Elizabeth's household. He was involved in the Wyatt rebellion and is known to have carried at least one message from Wyatt to the princess. Sir William was arrested, placed in the Tower and in June 1554 transferred to the Fleet prison. After paying £200 as surety for his future good conduct, like Courtenay, he was released in 1555. He was to perform an important role as Captain of the Queen's Guard at Elizabeth I's coronation and became Chief Butler of England. He sat in Elizabeth's second parliament as an MP for Derbyshire and became a JP for the county. Sir William settled Bess's debt to the Crown, reduced to £1,000 by Queen Elizabeth. He died in December 1565. At the time of his death, his brother, Edward, was in London, the brothers being engaged in bitter dispute over the future of their father's estates.[78]

If there was a scheme to plant Cavendish in Derbyshire its continuing success was brought to a temporary halt by his death in 1557. Bess's third husband, Sir William St Loe, was himself part of the wider Grey affinity. Should Sir William die without issue, his heir was his brother Edward who along with their sister Elizabeth had been excluded from their father's will.[79] Sir William's first wife was Jane, daughter of Sir Edward Baynton. Neighbours of the St Loes, the Thynnes and the Seymours, the Bayntons were the largest landowners in the area and supporters of evangelical reform. Sir Edward became vice-chamberlain to Anne Boleyn and a close ally of Hugh Latimer.[80] Both Sir Edward and Sir John St Loe were among the guests at the christening of Edward VI.[81] Jane died in 1549. The marriage produced no children.[82] Having conceived eight times during her ten years of marriage to Cavendish, Bess had amply demonstrated her fecundity. Perhaps St Loe hoped Bess would provide him with an heir. But, if he needed an heir, why would he have waited some ten years before his second marriage? Edward St Loe appears to have been sufficiently alarmed at the prospect of his brother's marriage to Bess producing an heir that he allegedly turned to desperate measures to prevent it. In addition to claims of the use of sorcery, in a letter to Bess dated June 1560, the brothers' stepmother, Margaret St Loe, claimed that she had been informed by an anonymous lady that shortly after St Loe's marriage Edward had attempted to poison both Bess and his brother. The accusation of attempted murder was investigated but presumably due to a lack of evidence, substance or both, Edward was never convicted of the offence. St Loe's marriage to Bess proved childless. It has been claimed that Edward's alleged attempt to commit double murder so embittered Sir William that, despite Bess's reluctance, in his will Sir William left all his lands, possessions and wealth, to her. He was free to do so because the lands had not been settled after his father's death.[83] By cutting out Edward from his will Sir William merely reaffirmed the provisions of his father's will.[84]

Twice widowed, with six children to bring up and a huge debt hanging over her head, Bess might not have been considered the most attractive prospect for a bride. On the other hand, William St Loe must have been an attractive prospect as a husband. In order to explain why he married Bess various authors have argued that, like Cavendish before him, St Loe simply loved her, a conclusion based mainly on the expressions of love and affection he used in the small number of his letters that survive.[85] However, caution must be exercised when interpreting such expressions as being matters of fact rather than of convention.[86] The St Loes were well known to Sir William Cavendish and Bess through his associations with Edward Seymour, the Greys, the Parrs, the Thynnes and others both inside and outside court circles.

Sir William's marriage to Margaret Bostock had produced two daughters. Catherine and Anne. Catherine married Thomas Brooke, son of Lord Cobham, whose sister, Elizabeth, was William Parr's second wife. Anne married Henry Baynton, brother of Sir William St Loe's first wife, Jane Baynton.[87] William Cavendish was therefore related by marriage to the St Loes sometime before his marriage to Bess which indicates that William St Loe and Bess must have known each other long before they married in 1559. Bess faced a desperate situation at the time of her marriage to St Loe. Possibly encouraged by Sir John Thynne, Sir William's marriage to Bess may have been little more than an act of kindness by one old friend to another. St Loe and Bess spent relatively little time together during their six-year marriage. Sir William's position at court necessitated his presence in London whereas Bess spent much of their marriage at Chatsworth. However, St Loe's marriage to Bess helped to re-establish the Grey affinity's presence in Derbyshire. The wedding of Lady Katherine Grey to Somerset's son, Edward, earl of Hertford, in December 1560 took place during the period of the St Loe marriage and reflected the continuing concerns of the Grey affinity, now headed by George Talbot, 6th earl of Shrewsbury. No-one could predict how long Elizabeth might reign. Should she die without issue Katherine was a potential successor. Elizabeth's near death from smallpox in October 1562,[88] was a sharp reminder, if one was needed, that the threat of a Catholic succession had not entirely evaporated with Queen Mary's death.

This concern may also have been a factor in Bess's fourth marriage to George Talbot, whose family was closely aligned with the Greys, Willoughbys, Parrs, Herberts and other leading members of the affinity. Talbot's father, Francis, 5th Earl of Shrewsbury, was among the signatories of Edward VI's 'devise'[89] but not closely allied to Northumberland. In 1562, the 6th earl's eldest son, Francis, Lord Talbot, married Anne, daughter of William Herbert, 1st earl of Pembroke, and Anne Parr, sister of Catherine Parr. Within months of Bess becoming widowed for the third time court gossip buzzed with rumours of potential suitors, Sir John Thynne, Lord Darcy and Sir Henry Cobham, being the main contenders,[90] but within a few months of the death of his first wife, Gertrude Manners, George Talbot, 6th earl of Shrewsbury, married Bess. Unlike Cavendish and St Loe there can be no suggestion of the earl needing a male heir as he already had his 'heir and spare' in Francis, Lord Talbot, and Gilbert Talbot. He was vastly wealthier than Bess. Adding her wealth to his own cannot have been the sole motive for their marriage. The earl would have had control of Bess's Cavendish and St Loe estates during their marriage but Bess held only a life interest in the Cavendish lands, which had been settled mainly on Henry Cavendish in 1557, and her St Loe estates passed to Charles Cavendish. As with St Loe's marriage to Bess, Talbot's marriage to Bess served to maintain the political and religious presence in north Derbyshire that had been established in 1547 by the Greys via Sir William Cavendish's marriage to Bess. Mary, Queen of Scots, was not placed in the custody of George Talbot in 1569 solely because he was a person of great wealth, nor just because Mary would be held at properties far distant from court, but also because by that time Talbot had become the leading member of a significant Protestant affinity, the origins of which lay in the extension of royal authority following the Pilgrimage of Grace and on which Elizabeth and her government believed they could depend.

E. W. Ives dedicated his biography of Lady Jane Grey 'To my many friends who have grappled with the reign of Edward VI'. Finding one's way through the maze of high politics during the mid-sixteenth century remains challenging. Following the failure to place Jane on the throne, many of the leaders of the attempt, such as Henry Grey, escaped with their lives, at least for the time being. Shamelessly yet pragmatically, former allies left John Dudley[91] to his fate on Tower Hill where he was beheaded in August 1553. Early in Elizabeth's reign an anonymous account characterised Somerset as the 'good duke' and Northumberland as his evil counterpart.[92] Dudley became a scapegoat and dead men cannot defend themselves. Inevitably, much that could have been used to convict others disappeared at the time, shortly afterwards or in the years that followed. Sir William Cavendish had witnessed first-hand the fall of powerful men such as Wolsey, Cromwell and Somerset. Men like Cavendish, operating a tier or so below the principal members of the aristocratic affinities they served, were clever, astute, careful and cautious. They understood the dangers that letters and papers might pose in any given circumstance and they were adept at covering their tracks. Thus far, it has proved impossible to discover documentary evidence of any involvement many such men may have had in events such as the attempt to prevent Mary Tudor's accession and her marriage to Philip of Spain. We should not be surprised by this paucity of evidence and accept that much must be inferred.

Conclusions reached in these circumstances are necessarily speculative yet remain worthy of consideration.

Placing Sir William Cavendish's marriage to Bess against the backdrop of the economic and political upheavals of the mid-sixteenth century makes it possible to take into account previously unconsidered factors which not only help to explain the marriage itself but additionally Sir William's subsequent decision to relocate to Derbyshire. It is an explanation in which Bess can be seen not as a force for unbridled dynastic ambition but as a pawn in the politico-religious manoeuvres of powerful aristocratic affinities.

REFERENCES & NOTES:

[1] *The Works of Horatio Walpole, Earl of Orford* (London, 1798), IV, 206. My thanks are extended to Peter Foden, my friend and former colleague, Lesley. A. Bilby and to Philip Riden, for helpful comments and proof-reading skills.

[2] Sir William Dugdale, *Baronage of England* (London, 1675–6), 420.

[3] E. Lodge, *Illustrations of British History*, (London, 1838), I, p. xxviii.

[4] T. Kilburn, 'The wardship and marriage of Robert Barley, first husband of Bess of Hardwick', *Derbyshire Archaeological Journal*, 134 (2014), 197–203.

[5] P. Riden, 'Sir William Cavendish: Tudor civil servant and founder of a dynasty', *Derbyshire Archaeological Journal*, 129 (2009), 248.

[6] Riden, *ibid*, 224.

[7] A. Collins, *Historical Collections of the Noble Families of Cavendishe, Holles, Vere, Harley and Ogle*, (London, 1752), 22.

[8] Collins, *Historical Collections* 10; Riden, 'Cavendish', 224.

[9] D. MacCulloch, *Thomas Cromwell: A Life* (London: Allen Lane, 2018), 549.

[10] The National Archives (TNA) STAC 3/1/49.

[11] Riden, 'Cavendish', 245.

[12] A.C. Jones, 'Commotion Time: the English risings of 1549' (Unpublished PhD thesis, University of Warwick, 2003), 33–4, 40 n. 22.

[13] Riden, 'Cavendish', 247.

[14] J. Loach and R. Tittler (eds), *Problems in Focus: The Mid-Tudor Polity, c.1540–1560* (London: MacMillan, 1980) provides a useful introduction.

[15] M. Scard, *Edward Seymour, Lord Protector: Tudor king in all but name* (Stroud: History Press, 2016), 161, 266 n. 30.

[16] Loach and Tittler (eds), *Mid-Tudor Policy*, 34–5.

[17] C. Skidmore, *Edward VI: the lost king of England* (London: Weidenfield & Nicolson, 2007), 183; J.E. Neale, *Queen Elizabeth I* (London, 1979), 378.

[18] Kilburn, 'Wardship', 195.

[19] TNA, C 1/1101/17; Kilburn, *ibid*, 201, n. 17.

[20] Kilburn, *ibid*, 198–9.

[21] Collins, *Historical Collections,*, 11, 19.

[22] Collins, *Historical Collection,* 19–20. Sir William and Bess's second son was probably named in honour of Charles Brandon and their third William, if not named after his father may well have been named for William Parr.

[23] D. Ashead and D.A.H.B. Taylor (eds), *Hardwick Hall: a great old castle of romance* (New Haven and London: Yale University Press, 2016), 73, citing Devonshire MSS, H/143/6; Durant, 52.

[24] V. Wilson, *Queen Elizabeth's Maids of Honour* (London: Bodley Head, 1922), 27.

[25] D.M. Durant, *Bess of Hardwick: portrait of an Elizabethan Dynast* (London: Weidenfield & Nicholson, 1979), 12. There is no evidence to support Dugdale's claim that Bess entered the service of the Zouches of Codnor and none to confirm her service with the Greys; P. Riden, 'The Hardwicks of Hardwick Hall in the fifteenth and sixteenth centuries', *Derbyshire Archaeological Journal*, 130 (2010), 152.

[26] Riden, 'Hardwicks', 157

[27] TNA, STAC 2/17/53.

[28] Riden, 'Hardwicks' 147. The suggestion that Bess's link to the Greys came about via her association with the Willoughbys is, in my view, much more probable that the notion that it was due to Bess's extremely distant relationship to the Greys of Sandiacre.

[29] Riden, 'Cavendish', 239; Bath Mss, Thynne Mss. 2, ff. 250-253v.; *History of Parliament. Commons 1509–58*, Sir William Cavendish.

[30] G. White, '"that whycheysnedefoulle and nesesary": the nature and purpose of the original furnishing and decoration of Hardwick Hall' (Unpublished PhD thesis, University of Warwick, 2005), 293, 468.

[31] Riden, 'Cavendish', 239–40.

[32] *History of Parliament. Commons 1509–58*, Sir William Cavendish.

[33] Durant, *Bess of Hardwick: portrait of an Elizabethan dynast*, 26–7.

[34] *ibid*, 47.

[35] *ibid*, 16.

[36] Scard, *Seymour*, 17.

[37] E.W. Ives, *Lady Jane Grey: a Tudor Mystery* (Oxford: Wiley-Blackwell, 2011), 43–5.

[38] S. Gunn, *Charles Brandon*: *Henry VIII's closest friend*, (Stroud: Amberley, 2015), 157.

[39] Ives, *Lady Jane Grey*, 184.

[40] Scard, *Seymour*, 119–20.

[41] Neale, *Elizabeth I*, ch. 2; Scard, *Seymour*, 120–5; J. Loach, *Edward VI*, (New Haven and London: Yale University Press, 1999), 56–7.

[42] Neale, *Elizabeth I*, 29–33.

[43] D.E. Hoak, *The King's Council in the Reign of Edward VI* (Cambridge: Cambridge University Press, 1976), 96–7; Scard, *Seymour*, 74, 154; S.R. Gammon, *Statesman and Schemer: William First Lord Paget, Tudor Minister* (Newton Abbot: David & Charles, 1973), 152.

[44] *History of Parliament. Commons 1558–1603*, John Thynne.

[45] Beer. B.L, 'Edward, duke of Somerset [known as Protector Somerset] (c.1500–1552)', *Oxford Dictionary of National Biography*, https://doi.org/10.1093/ref:odnb/25159; J. North (ed), *England's Boy King: the diary of Edward VI, 1547– 1553* (Welwyn Garden City: Ravenhall Books, 2005), 40; Scard, *Seymour*, 124.

[46] L. Boynton, *The Hardwick Hall Inventories of 1601* (London: Furniture History Society, 1971), 29.

[47] Scard, *Seymour*, 230; Loach, *Edward VI*, 93; Skidmore, *Edward VI*, 207–9.

[48] *History of Parliament. Commons 1558–1603*, Sir John St Loe.

[49] Skidmore, *Edward VI*, 191–2; Gammon, 178–9; Scard, *Seymour*, 225.

[50] J.G. Nichols (ed.), *The Chronicle of Queen Jane and Queen Mary* (Camden Society, Old Series 48, 1850), 7, 10.

[51] Riden, 'Cavendish', 247; Durant, 26.

[52] *History of Parliament. Commons 1509–58*, Sir William Cavendish.

[53] D. Loades, *Mary Tudor* (Oxford: Blackwell, 1989), 190.

[54] *History of Parliament. Commons 1509–58*, Sir William Cavendish.

[55] TNA, E 101/424/10, *History of Parliament. Commons 1509–58*, Sir William Cavendish.

[56] Riden, 'Cavendish', 247–8.

[57] Collins, *Historical Collections*, 20.

[58] *ibid*, 12.

[59] *ibid*, 19-20; Durant, *Bess of Hardwick*, 20–7. If William was not named after his father a likely candidate for this honour is William Parr whose wife, Elizabeth Brooke, stood as one of William's godmothers and was godmother to Sir William and Bess's daughter Elizabeth.

[60] I am indebted to Peter Foden for advising me that In a box labelled 'pedigrees' in the Belvoir Castle Muniments there is a book of manuscript pedigrees of *c.*1565. The unknown genealogist was trying to explain contemporary allegiances. Among the pedigrees is one titled 'Leeke Grey and Frechvyle'.

[61] See generally S. M. Wright, *The Derbyshire Gentry in the Fifteenth Century* (Derbyshire Record Society, 1983).

[62] MacCulloch, *Cromwell*, 272–5, 435.

[63] Durant, *Bess,* 18-19.

[64] Durant, *ibid*, 23; Riden, 'Cavendish', 245–7.

[65] Gammon, *'Statesman and Schemer'*, 179–80.

[66] Riden, 'Cavendish', 247.

[67] I am grateful to Peter Foden for this information.

[68] Scard, *Seymour*, 82–3.

[69] Nichols, *Chronicle*, 89–91; J. G. Nichols (ed.), *Literary Remains of King Edward the Sixth*, (Roxburghe Club, 1857), 571–3.

[70] Riden, 'Cavendish', 247.

[71] White, "that whycheysnedefoulle and nesesary", Appendix One, 1540s Inventory of Northaw, 324, among Sir William's possession were at that time a mixture of items belonging to the catholic faith and a vernacular bible, probably Coverdale's 1539 Great Bible.

[72] Ives, *Jane Grey,* 185.

[73] Loades, *Mary Tudor*, 179.

[74] *History of Parliament. Commons 1558–1603*, Sir John St Loe; Sir William St Loe; P.Riden, 'Bess of Hardwick and the St Loe Inheritance' in P. Riden and D. G. Edwards (eds), *Essays in Derbyshire History Presented to Gladwyn Turbutt* (Derbyshire Record Society, 30, 2006), 80–106.

[75] *History of Parliament. Commons 1558–1603*, Sir John St Loe, 330.

[76] W.H. Stevenson, *Report on the Manuscripts of Lord Middleton*, HMSO, 1911, 415.

[77] *History of Parliament. Commons 1558–1603*, Sir John St Loe, 260.

[78] Riden, 'St Loe inheritance', 100–102.

[79.] Riden, *ibid*, 95.

[80] MacCulloch, *Cromwell*, 167.

[81] https://www.british-history.ac.uk/letters-papers-hen8/vol12/no2/320.

[82] G.W. Marshall (ed.), *The Visitation of Wiltshire, 1623* (London: Bell, 1882), 8, 44, 37, 54; Lodge, *Illustrations*, I, p. xxviii, stated that Sir William St Loe had 'daughters by a former wife' but does not say how many daughters; Riden, 'St Loe inheritance', 98, n 7. The St Loe pedigree lists Sir William as *ob. s.p. (obit sine prole)*, that is 'died without issue'. No children are mentioned in his will. However, it was not unusual for a spouse to refer to children from a previous marriage as being their own children. St Loe referred to Bess's children as his children. At the time of his death two of Bess's daughters by Cavendish, Mary and Elizbeth, were yet to marry and it is likely that these are the two daughters that earlier authors were referring to when stating that St Loe had two daughters.

[83] TNA, PROB 11/48/200; TNA, C 3/170/13(2); Durant, *Bess,* 39.

[84] Riden, 'St Loe inheritance', 93; TNA, PROB 11/42B/241.

[85] See, for example, Durant, *Bess of Hardwick: portrait of an Elizabethan Dynast,* 35.

[86] For a discussion of 'courtly love' see E. W. Ives, *Anne Boleyn* (Oxford: Blackwell, 1986), 77–110.

[87] Collins, *Historical Collections,* 18-19.

[88] J. Hurstfield, *Elizabeth I and the Unity of England* (Harmondsworth: Penguin, 1971), 44–55; Neale, 123.

[89] Nichols, *Literary Remains*, 573 and n. 42.

[90] Durant, *Bess*, 53.

[91] Nichols, *The Chronicle of Queen Jane and Queen Mary*, 7, 10.

[92] A.J.A. Malkiewicz, 'An eye-witness's account of the coup d'état of October 1549', *English Historical Review*, 70 (1955), 600–9; C.L. Kingsford (ed), 'Two London chronicles from the collections of John Stowe', *Camden*

Miscellany, 4 (Camden Society, 3rd ser, 18, 1910), 17–43; A.F, Pollard. *England Under Protector Somerset*, (London: Kegan Paul, 1900), also presented Somerset as the 'good duke', as did W.K, Jordan, *Edward VI: the young king* (London: Allen and Unwin,1968). This was challenged by B.L. Beer in his *The Political Career of John Dudley, Earl of Warwick and Duke of Northumberland* (Kent State University Press, 1973) and in his 'Northumberland: the myth of the wicked duke and the historical John Dudley', *Albion*, 11 (1979), 1–14. See also D.E. Hoak, 'Rehabilitating the duke of Northumberland: politics and political control, 1549–155", in Loach and Tittler (eds), *Mid-Tudor Polity*, 29–51; M.L. Bush, *The Government Policy of Protector Somerset* (London: Edward Arnold, 1975), 160-161.

3

Hardwick's Sabine Tapestries

Helen Wyld and Terry Kilburn

a) The Reconciliation of Romulus and Titus Tatius

The following, written in collaboration with Dr Helen Wyld, can be found at http://www.nationaltrustcollections.org.uk/object/1129463.1

Hardwick Hall © National Trust / Robert Thrift

Summary

Tapestry, wool and silk, 7 warps per cm, The Reconciliation of Romulus and Titus Tatius from a series of four of the History of the Sabines, probably French, after a design probably by Claude Bosquet, c. 1694-1707. At the centre of the scene the two main figures embrace at the top of a set of stone steps leading onto a large stone paved area. On the left is the blue-cloaked Romulus, and on the right is the scarlet-cloaked Titus Tatius wearing a swan-crested helmet. Two other figures, a scarlet-cloaked Sabine soldier and blue-cloaked Roman soldier, stand facing each other to the centre right. The scene as a whole contains numerous men and women in happy interaction celebrating the end of hostilities and the on-set of peace. At the lower right a small child is depicted apparently holding hands with a woman wearing a red dress. Towards the background to the left of Romulus a woman holds a basket and distributes flowers. At bottom left a man stands with his right arm over a wooden fence. A kneeling figure bottom left holds a fasces (an axe tied to a bundles of sticks) and at the top right are various weapons of war, now redundant, placed between blue marble columns. In the background is a partially completed arched structure and to the left a tree in full foliage and a partially complete (or partially destroyed) obelisk. The tapestry has stone coloured borders with arabesque patterns, angels at the upper corners carrying plaques bearing the monogram of the Duke of Devonshire, roundels with profile heads at the centre of each side, sphinxes at the lower corners and swags of leaves and fruit at the top and bottom. At the bottom centre is a roundel with the Cavendish crest of an entwined serpent, and above this two-winged putti play with a leopard. The angel at the upper right carries an olive branch, signalling peace.

Full description

'The Reconciliation of Romulus and Titus Tatius' is the last of the four scenes from the 'History of the Sabines' at Hardwick. The war between Romulus and the Sabine king, Titus Tatius, was brought to an end by the intervention of the Sabine women who placed themselves and their children between the two opposing armies as they fought on ground between the Palatine and Capitoline hills. Thereafter, it was agreed that the two sets of people would live as one ruled jointly by Romulus and Titus Tatius. The tapestry shows the reconciliation between the two rulers. The swan-crested helmet and scarlet cloak worn by Titus Tatius are intended to represent his Spartan origin, the Sabines claiming descent from the Sparta. The same is true for the Sabine soldier shown to the right of Titus Tatius who is probably Mettius Curtius, the Sabine soldier who commanded the frontline against Romulus as the Romans launched their attempt to re-take the Capitoline citadel from the Sabines. The two leaders, Romulus and Titus Tatius, embrace each other while Mettius and a Roman counterpart engage in conversation. Elsewhere in the tapestry Romans and Sabines celebrate the cessation of hostilities and the union of their peoples. The Sabine women had married Roman men and borne them children. Interestingly, the composition of the tapestry includes only one child. The child depicted holds a woman's hand which may imply this woman is of some significance. It is possible that the woman is Hersilia. Plutarch says that some believed Hersilia was the wife of Hostilius whilst others thought her the wife of Romulus (Plutarch, Life of Romulus). He says that she was the only married woman taken during the abduction. Livy describes her as the wife of Romulus (Livy, History of Rome, I.11). It was Hersilia who led the women to intervene in the fighting and in so doing brought the war to an end. With the fighting at an end the abducted women were now able to introduce their Roman husbands and the offspring of their marriages to their Sabine families. The three 'Sabines' tapestries at Hardwick were long thought to represent the 'History of Alexander', and their place of production was uncertain. Their true subject was recently identified thanks to the swan-crested helmets and red cloaks of some of the soldiers, which according to ancient sources were worn by the Sabines to denote their Spartan heritage. This identification was confirmed by the discovery of two painted silk hangings which have similar borders to the tapestries at Hardwick, and which also show scenes from the History of the Sabines. The silk hangings were made for Louis XIV and may have served as models for the tapestries, making it probable that the tapestries were woven in France. The tapestries must have been commissioned by or for William Cavendish, 1st Duke of Devonshire (1641-1707), as they are woven with his arms, and are thus a rare example of French tapestries being commissioned by an English patron at a time when the two countries were in conflict. Research is still underway on the identity of the painter who designed the series, and the circumstances in which the tapestries were commissioned. The three tapestries at Hardwick include four scenes from the 'History of the Sabines': 'The Abduction of the Sabines' and 'The Retreat to the Palatine Gate' sewn together as one tapestry (1129463.3), 'Titus Tatius Attacking the Citadel' (1129463.2), and 'The Reconciliation of Romulus and Titus Tatius' (1129463.1). The main ancient sources for the story of the Sabines are Plutarch's 'Life of Romulus' and Livy's 'Early History of Rome'. The first event represented in the tapestries, the 'Abduction of the Sabines', is traditionally dated to 18 August, 750 BC, and, according to Fabrius, took place four months after the completion of the building of Rome. Following the establishment of Rome, a lack of brides for the men of the city forced the Roman ruler Romulus to seek inter-marriage treaties with neighbouring tribes. These tribes, including the Sabines, considered themselves to be descendants of Lacedaemonians, more commonly known as Spartans. Romulus' overtures were scornfully rejected leading him to adopt a more cunning and violent method of acquiring brides for the men of his city. Romulus announced that he had discovered an altar to a local underground god named either as the Equestrian Neptune or as Consus, a god of secret counsel after whom later 'consules' or counsellors were named. To celebrate his discovery Romulus presided over a special day of sacrifice, public games and entertainments, to which he invited people from the surrounding region to attend. At a given point during the proceedings, Romulus threw his purple cloak over his body. This was a signal for his men to draw their swords and abduct the Sabine women. This scene became a popular one for artists and tapestry makers and is represented both on a portion of a composite tapestry in the Duke's Room at Hardwick Hall (1129463.3) and is also the subject of one of two painted silk hangings that are related to the tapestries (see below). The abduction of the Sabine Women led to a series of wars the first of which was fought between Romulus and Acron, King of the Ceninenses, whom Romulus challenged to a duel. After killing Acron in single combat, the two armies fought a battle which resulted in victory for Romulus followed by the first ever Roman Triumph. A second war ensued between Romulus and the leaders of the Crustumini, the Antemnates, and the Fidenae, who jointly attacked Romulus but were defeated leading to Romulus' second Roman Triumph. It is possible that the second painted silk hanging (see below) depicts the meeting of Romulus and Acron. The remaining Sabine leaders looked to Titus Tatius, the Sabine King of Cures, to champion the Sabine cause, and his successful attack on the Capitoline Hill citadel is almost certainly the theme of no. 1129463.2. The left-hand part of the composite tapestry, no. 1129463.3, very probably represents the aftermath of a fierce battle between the Romans and Sabines between the Capitoline and Palatine hills, when Mettius Curtius chased the retreating Romans to the Palatine Gate. After a long period of fighting the war between Romulus and the Sabines was brought to an end with the famous intervention of the Sabine woman and their children who, it is said, walked onto the battleground and placed themselves between the opposing armies pleading with their fathers, brothers, uncles, husbands and in-laws to stop fighting each other. This in turn led to the reconciliation between Romulus and Titus Tatius which is the theme of the large tapestry on the half-landing at Hardwick Hall (1129463.1). Romulus and Titus Tatius agreed to rule Rome jointly and it is from this point in their history that the Romans and Sabines considered themselves to be a single people. The intervention of the Sabine women and their children brought a dramatic end to the conflict between Romulus and the Sabines. Again, this proved to be a popular theme for artists and tapestry makers. The surviving tapestries at Hardwick Hall do not include a depiction of this scene but the complete set may originally have done so. Other scenes which may have once formed part of a 'Sabine' series of tapestries possibly included a depiction of the fate of Tarpeia, the death of Hostus Hostilius and, possibly, the battlefield escape of Mettius Curtius. The designs of the four tapestries at Hardwick can be linked to two late seventeenth-century painted silk hangings which recently surfaced in an English private collection. The painted hangings show different scenes to the tapestries though their subjects are also drawn from the History of the Sabines. The painted silks share with the Hardwick tapestries the same distinctive borders with Caesars' heads and sphinxes at the sides, angels at the upper corners, and putti playing at the bottom centre. These borders do not appear on any other known tapestries or hangings. One of the painted silks clearly shows the 'Abduction of the Sabine Women', a subject also included in the tapestries at Hardwick, but the design is different. The second silk hanging shows a triumphal procession of soldiers on foot and horseback and may represent the Roman army after one of their victories over the Sabines. Whereas the Hardwick tapestries are woven with the arms and devices of William Cavendish, 1st Duke of Devonshire, the painted silks carry instead the French Royal arms and entwined letters 'L' (for Louis) in Greek and Latin, indicating French a royal commission. The painted silks are each signed 'Bosquet inventor' at the upper edge of the lower border. These features allow them to be identified with a set of four painted silks of the history of the Sabines by 'Bosquet' that appear in the inventory of Louis XIV at the Château du Val, near Saint-Germain, in 1672. The inventory entry reads as follows: "576 – Une petite tenture de tapisserie de peinture sur une estoffe de soye blanche à gros grains, faite à Marseilles par le Sr Bosquet, représentant l'Histoire des Sabines, contenant 17 aunes de cours, sur 3 aunes de hault, en quatre pieces doublés de toile blanche." [A small suite of tapestries painted on coarse silk cloth, made in Marseilles by Mr Bosquet, representing the History of the Sabines, 17 ells in length by 3 ells in height, in four pieces lined with white canvas] (Guiffrey 1885-6, vol. 2, p. 286). The identity of the 'Bosquet' who signed the two painted silk, and who is mentioned in the 1672 inventory, is open to question as no forename is given in either source. He may be identical with an artist named 'Du Bosquet' who was paid 6,000 livres in 1677 for a portrait of Louis XIV and a number of other works, which may have included the painted silks (Chastagnol and Vittet 2013, p. 69). Three separate artists named Bosquet are recorded in the period, all of whom were active in Provence in southern France. A Clair Bosquet was living in Toulon in 1646, however no works are known by him (Alauzen 2006, p. 78). A painter named Jean Bosquet, from Moustiers, was recorded in Aix-en-Provence in 1665 and 1666, but again no works by him are recorded (Meissner 1992, p. 464; Boyer 1971, p. 91). Finally, a Claude Bosquet was active in Marseilles and Le Var from the 1660s to the 1680s. In 1663 he painted a 'Presentation of the Virgin' for a church in the village of La Penne sur Huveaune; in 1666 an 'Assumption' for the church of Cuers; and in 1684 the City of Marseilles commissioned from him a now lost portrait of the King. In 1682 he acted as a guarantor for the painter Michel Serre (1658-1733), who had arrived in Marseilles to paint murals at the Convent of the Minimes without being a member of the city's guild (Homet 1987, pp. 56, 166, 180 n. 53, 187). One painting by Claude Bosquet survives: the 'Presentation of the Virgin', which remains in the Church of Saint-Laurent, La-Penne-sur-Huveaune, a small village to the east of Marseilles. The painting is signed 'Bosquet inventor 1663' – using the same slightly unusual form of words as the signatures on the two painted silk hangings of the Sabines, which also read 'Bosquet inventor'. Stylistic features also suggest that the La Penne painting and the painted hangings could be by the same hand, allowing a tentative attribution of the painted silks, and thus potentially the design of the Hardwick tapestries, to Claude Bosquet. The relationship between the painted silks made for Louis XIV and the Hardwick tapestries is not entirely clear, but since they have the same borders (which are not known to appear anywhere else), and share a common subject of the History of the Sabines, it is probable that all six scenes are part of a single design series. One possible scenario is that the Hardwick tapestries were woven using the painted silks as models or cartoons; this is quite possible since both paintings and tapestries are roughly the same height. All three tapestries bear the arms and monograms of William Cavendish, 1st Duke of Devonshire (1641-1707) allowing them to be dated to between 1694, when he was created Duke, and 1707, when he died. Since the painted silks were in the French Royal collection until at least the 1720s (information kindly supplied by Jean Vittet), the tapestries were very probably woven in France. The principal French workshop in the period was the Manufacture Royale des Gobelins in Paris, established as a Royal manufactory in 1667 by incorporating existing Parisian workshops. The Gobelins worked principally for the King, although commissions were executed for other prominent clients. It is unlikely that the Hardwick tapestries were an official product of the Gobelins as they are not signed but the workshops there are known to have woven unofficial works as well. Moreover, the Gobelins was officially closed from 1694-1699 due to restricted crown finances resulting from European military campaigns, and in this period production continued, but the works were often unsigned. In addition to the Gobelins, other small workshops were operating in Paris between 1694 and 1707, some of them manned by ex-Gobelins weavers, and one of these could have been responsible for the Hardwick tapestries. As noted above the tapestries bear the arms and personal devices of William Cavendish, 1st Duke of Devonshire (1641-1707). His coat of arms, complete with Ducal coronet and Garter, and the Cavendish motto 'Cavendo Tutus' (safety through caution) appear at the top centre of each tapestry. The angels at the upper corners carry plaques bearing his monogram, 'WDD' for William, Duke of Devonshire, also crowned with a Ducal coronet, and the Cavendish crest of an entwined serpent appears in a roundel at the bottom centre, again crowned with the Ducal coronet. Less easy to explain are the pairs of putti playing with leopards directly above the roundels. In the painted silks the boys are playing with a lion, probably a reference to frequent comparisons of King Louis XIV with a lion. It is possible that the replacement of a lion with a leopard in the Duke of Devonshire's tapestries was related to his membership of a drinking club called the Honourable Order of Little Bedlam, founded by the Earl of Exeter in 1684, which met at Burghley House. Each member of the club was known by the name of an animal, and the Duke of Devonshire was The Leopard (RCHM 1876, p. 399). In his 'Handbook of Chatsworth and Hardwick' (1844), the 6th Duke of Devonshire's notes that: "The tapestry on the lower staircase came from Chatsworth: that with arms and ducal coronets hung in the Leicester apartments there" (Cavendish 1844,

p. 187). This almost certainly refers to the 'Sabines' which is the only set now at Hardwick (or indeed Chatsworth) to have arms and ducal coronets.

b) Titus Tatius's Attack on the Citadel

The following, written in collaboration with Dr Helen Wyld, can be found at http://www.nationaltrustcollections.org.uk/object/1129463.2

Hardwick Hall © National Trust / Robert Thrift

Summary

Tapestry, wool and silk, 7 warps per cm, The Reconciliation of Romulus and Titus Tatius from a set of three of the History of the Sabines, probably French, after a design probably by Claude Bosquet, c. 1694-1707. The main figure, on horseback in the foreground, wears a swan-crested helmet and a scarlet cloak and tunic. He leads his army in an attack on a large building with columns and pedimented roof depicted on the left-hand side. He holds a gold baton in his left hand and the horse's reins in his right hand. To the bottom left a soldier is about to be trampled by the main figure's horse. Behind the main figure are infantry and cavalry: three soldiers are on horseback three soldiers follow behind the main figure to the right blowing battle horns, and further soldiers to the right carry weapons and regalia. There are trees in full foliage in the background. The tapestry has stone coloured borders with arabesque patterns, angels at the upper corners carrying plaques bearing the monogram of the Duke of Devonshire, roundels with profile heads at the centre of each side, sphinxes at the lower corners and swags of leaves and fruit at the top and bottom. At the bottom centre is a roundel with the Cavendish crest of an entwined serpent, and above this two-winged putti play with a leopard. The angel at the upper right carries a curved horn, the same instrument carried by the soldiers in the main scene.

Description

'Titus Tatius's Attack on the Citadel' is the second of four scenes from the 'History of the Sabines' at Hardwick. The main figure depicted in this tapestry is the Sabine king, Titus Tatius. He wears the swan-crested helmet and scarlet tunic and cloak intended to represent his Spartan descent. At the start of the hostilities with Romulus, Titus Tatius attacked the citadel on the Capitoline Hill, the building shown on the left in the tapestry in which the Sabine soldiers on the right sound the attack with their battle horns. Titus Tatius gained control of the citadel partly through the treachery of Tarpaia, the daughter of Tarpeius, the Roman Captain of the Citadel. Tarpeia had come out of the citadel to collect water and was bribed by Titus Tatius. She agreed to open the gates to the citadel for the Sabines in return for "What they had on their shield-arms" (Livy, History of Rome, I.11). Tarpeia hoped for the gold bracelets they wore on their left arms but she was crushed to death under the weight of the shields that the Sabines wore strapped to their left arms. Plutarch tells us that Titus Tatius first threw his gold bracelet and buckler at Tarpeia and then his shield (Plutarch, Life of Romulus). The remaining Sabine soldiers followed suit with their shields and in this way Tarpeia received a reward she was certainly not expecting. In later times, those who betrayed Rome were cast from the rock which bore her name, the Tarpeian Rock.

c) The Retreat to the Palatine Gate and the Abduction of the Sabines

The following, written in collaboration with Dr Helen Wyld, can be found at http://www.nationaltrustcollections.org.uk/object/1129463.3

Hardwick Hall © National Trust / Robert Thrift

Summary

Tapestry, wool and silk, 7 warps per cm, The Retreat to the Palatine Gate and the Abduction of the Sabines, from a set of three of the History of the Sabines, probably French, after a design probably by Claude Bosquet, c. 1694-1707. This piece consists of two tapestries with different scenes that have been sewn together. On the left is a narrow vertical scene, clearly part of a larger design, probably representing the 'Retreat to the Palatine Gate'. In the foreground a number of soldiers moving in a generally right to left direction. The soldier in the foreground wears a red tunic and a purple cuirass and carries a curved sword in his left hand. Behind this soldier another, dressed in a blue/white tunic and red cloak, waves a blue and white pennant in his left hand and carries a shield. Behind this last and to his left a soldier carries a pinkish flag. Another carries a military standard. Two soldiers are looking back to where the foreleg of a horse can just be seen centre right. In the background there is a structure with a pediment and a vista through an open archway. The larger, right-hand scene shows the 'Abduction of the Sabine Women'. In what could be described as a chaotic scene, terrified women can be seen being forcibly taken and carried off in the arms of men whilst others attempt to fend off their attackers. To the left a man carries of a woman in his arms and at lower centre another woman falls to her knees as she attempts to fend off her abductor. Ten faces can be counted of which five appear to be men and five women. In the background on the right is a structure with three columns. The upper background shows two trees in full foliage and beyond these a view into the distance where on the left there is what appears to be some form of man-made structure, perhaps a distant village or town. The tapestry has stone coloured borders with arabesque patterns, angels at the upper corners carrying plaques bearing the monogram of the Duke of Devonshire, roundels with profile heads at the centre of each side, sphinxes at the lower corners and swags of leaves and fruit at the top and bottom. The angel at the top left carries an olive branch, emblem of peace. Although the two scenes are incomplete the edges of borders are visible at the join in the centre, indicating that the tapestries were woven with the main scenes as they now appear, probably from more extensive cartoons.

Description

The left hand of the two scenes in the tapestry may represent 'The Retreat to the Palatine Gate', making it the third of four scenes from the 'History of the Sabines' at Hardwick. The Romans attempted to re-take the citadel on the Capitoline Hill from the Sabines, and they were met with fierce resistance. The Sabine frontline was led by Mettius Curtius and the Roman frontline by Hostius Hostilius. Hostilius was slain during the ensuing battle. According to Plutarch, at around the same time that Hostilius met his death Romulus was hit by a stone. The fall of Hostilius and the injury to Romulus caused panic to spread among the Romans and carrying Romulus they fled in retreat to the Palatine Gate with Mettius Curtius and the Sabines in hot pursuit. The

Romans were chased right up to the Palatine Gate itself when Romulus, recovered from his injury, rallied his soldiers and launched a counterattack during which Mettius Curtius's horse became bogged down in a morass and Mettius himself was fortunate to escape the battlefield with his life. It may well be that the chase to the Palatine Gate is the subject of the partial section of tapestry in the Duke's Room at Hardwick, the background structure being the Palatine Gate. In this case, the rider of the unseen horse would be Mettius Curtius. It is likely that the soldiers depicted are Sabines in pursuit of the retreating Romans. The sword which the soldier in the fore-ground carries may be a kopsis, a curved sword used by Spartans as a secondary weapon for hacking down opponents. The right-hand scene is easier to identify, and clearly depicts 'The Abduction of the Sabine Women'. This is the first scene from the 'History of the Sabines' at Hardwick. According to Livy's account, Romulus was acutely aware of the fledgling Rome's shortage of young woman to become wives, a situation that was blamed on the unwillingness of Rome's neighbours to allow inter-marriage. His efforts to secure treaties allowing inter-marriage with neighbouring states were rejected. He decided to hold a 'Consualia', a festival in honour of 'Equestrian Neptune', and he invited those from neighbouring states to attend (Livy, History of Rome, 1:9). Plutarch tells us that this happened on the 18th day of the month of Sextilis [August] and modern historians date the event to c.750 BC (Plutarch, Life of Romulus). The crowds assembled for the festivities. Romulus had armed his men and at a given signal they set upon the gathering and "ravished away the daughters of the Sabines." Livy simply states that they took all the young women each being the prize of whosoever took her. Romulus gave a speech in which he blamed the whole event on their fathers for having refused his offers of inter-marriage treaties and he encouraged the women to accept their new station in life as wives of Romans. Plutarch noted that it was in memory of the abduction of the Sabine women that the practice emerged of carrying newly married brides over the thresholds of their husbands' houses.

4

Three Into Two Won't Go: Marriage and Hardwick's 'Eglantine Table'

© National Trust Images/Robert Thrift

In 1601, Elizabeth, Dowager Countess of Shrewsbury, had inventories drawn up of the contents of her properties including the 'old' and 'new' halls at Hardwick. 'Bess of Hardwick', as the Countess is better known to history, was by that date in her eighties and preparing to make her will.[1] There is no specific reference to an 'Eglantine Table' in the 1601 inventories but in the High Great Chamber of the new hall the inventory clerk did list "a long table of white wood" and this is assumed to be the table now known as the 'Eglantine Table'.[2]

The 'Eglantine Table', which dates from around 1568, is still to be found in the High Great Chamber of Derbyshire's Hardwick Hall. It is often asserted that it was commissioned by Bess to commemorate three marriages:

that of Bess herself, to George Talbot, Earl of Shrewsbury, and two others involving four of their children.[3] The precise date and place of Bess's marriage to Talbot is not known.[4] All Bess's children had been fathered by her second husband, Sir William Cavendish, and the earl's six children were the issue of his first marriage to Gertrude, Lady Manners. On the 9th of February 1568, the earl's youngest daughter, 8-year-old Grace Talbot, was married to Bess's eldest son, Henry Cavendish, the 17-year-old heir of Sir William. At the same time, the earl's 15-year-old second son, Gilbert, married Bess's youngest daughter, Mary Cavendish, who was 12. It has been suggested that the marriages of the children came about at Bess's instigation but such a strategy of multiple-marriage was commonplace among the Elizabethan aristocracy and had, for example, been pursued by Talbot himself in 1562 on the occasion of the marriage of his eldest son Francis which brought together the Talbot family and that of the Herberts, earls of Pembroke. Francis married Anne Herbert, eldest daughter of William Herbert, earl of Pembroke, and Anne Parr, younger sister of Catherine Parr. At the same time, Pembroke's son and heir, Henry Herbert, married George Talbot's eldest daughter, Catherine Talbot. Gilbert and Mary's daughter, the diminutive Mary Talbot, married William Herbert, 3rd earl of Pembroke, and became Countess of Pembroke.

The most important piece of evidence we have regarding the 'Eglantine Table' and its relationship to these marriages is the table itself. Inlaid into the top of the table are images of items such as playing cards, musical instruments, and various other pleasures and pastimes and popular during the Elizabethan age. Also inlaid into the top of the table are two heraldic marriage impalements. As viewed, such impalements depict the arms of the male to the left and the female to the right.[5] The first of the impalements depicts the arms of Talbot impaling those of Hardwick, obviously intended to represent the marriage of the earl to Bess. The second depicts the arms of Cavendish impaling those of Talbot, an unequivocal reference to the marriage of Henry Cavendish to Grace Talbot. Completely absent from the 'Eglantine Table' is any reference whatsoever to the marriage of Gilbert Talbot and Mary Cavendish.

If, as is often claimed, Hardwick's 'Eglantine Table' was indeed commissioned to commemorate *three* marriages, why there is no heraldic marriage impalement to represent a third marriage, the marriage of Gilbert Talbot and Mary Cavendish ? Is this merely an error, an oversight, or did the very highly skilled men who crafted the table simply have a lapse of memory and forgot to include a third heraldic impalement ? Or, was it possibly omitted because there was insufficient space for its inclusion ? Even to begin to contemplate such explanations is to stretch credulity to breaking point. There can be only one logical explanation for the omission: the 'Eglantine Table' was never intended to commemorate a third marriage. As evidenced by the two marriage impalements inlaid into the table itself demonstrate, the 'Eglantine Table' was commissioned to commemorate *two* marriages, not three.

Rank and position mattered to the Elizabethans and Bess was certainly status conscious. Among the more obvious examples of this are the huge 'ES' monograms that top Hardwick's lofty towers. Bess also chose to frame the non-aristocratic Hardwick coat of arms with heraldic supporters and to display monograms and the Hardwick arms beneath the coronet of a countess. Like the Eglantine Table, the Artemesia panel, one of what was once a set of five wall-hangings made at Chatsworth *c*. 1573, displays impalements depicting Bess's marriage to George Talbot and Henry Cavendish's marriage to Grace Talbot.[6] The over-mantle in the Cut Velvet Room provides a further example in its depictions of the marriage impalements of all six of Bess's surviving children, three to the left and three to the right. These are not placed in any chronological order beyond that of rank with each side being headed by one of Bess's two daughters who became countesses: Mary, Countess of Shrewsbury, and Elizabeth, Countess of Lennox. Bess continued to style herself 'Countess of Shrewsbury' until her own death on the 13th of February 1608, a confusing situation which led to both Bess and her daughter, Mary, being addressed as 'Countess of Shrewsbury' simultaneously.

We may wonder why Bess chose not to include the marriage of Gilbert Talbot and Mary Cavendish when she commissioned the table.[7] When the three marriages took place, Gilbert's elder brother, Francis, Lord Talbot, was still alive. Married to the daughter of the earl of Pembroke in 1562, Francis did not die until 1582. Gilbert was the 'spare' and not the 'heir'. In an Elizabethan aristocratic household, the first-born male was considered the most important followed by daughters who on marriage could be expected to attract substantial dowries. As a 15-year-old second son Gilbert's marriage to Mary was advantageous to both his father and to Bess. It strengthened further the ties between the Talbot and Cavendish families and it has been argued marriage to Gilbert conveniently relieved Bess of the necessity of providing Mary with a dowry. In terms of status, however, Gilbert and Mary's marriage was simply not in the same league as the marriages of Bess and her eldest son.

Once embedded into a narrative, it becomes notoriously difficult to dislodge historical myths. Does Hardwick's 'Eglantine Table' commemorate three marriages ? Put simply, three into two won't go !

REFERENCES & NOTES:

[1] The building of Hardwick New Hall commenced within weeks of the death of George Talbot who died on the 18th of November 1590. Modern biographers tend to give Bess' year of birth as 1527 but contemporary evidence suggests that a date of 1522/3 is more likely. For a discussion of Bess' year of birth see Philip Riden's 'The Hardwicks of Hardwick Hall in the Fifteenth and Sixteenth Centuries', *Derbyshire Archaeological Journal*, 130, (2010) 150-151.

[2] Boynton. L. (Ed), *The Hardwick Hall Inventories of 1601*, (1971), 27. The inventory also refers to a long, carved and inlaid, table in the Low Great Chamber. At Hardwick Hall is an Elizabethan inlaid table the central feature of which is interestingly a single heraldic marriage impalement, that of Talbot impaling Hardwick. Though obviously representing the marriage of Bess to George Talbot, it is not known who commissioned this table.

[3] Remarkably like Hardwick's 'Eglantine Table' is the 'Brome Table', part of Glasgow Museums' Burrell Collection. Dated 1569, the 'Brome Table' was also commissioned to commemorate marriage.

[4] Goldring. E., 'Talbot, Elizabeth [Bess of Hardwick], Countess of Shrewsbury (1527 ?–1608)' *Oxford Dictionary of National Biography*, Oxford University Press, 2004 [http://www.oxforddnb.com/view/article/26925]: Goldring. E., 'Talbot, George, sixth earl of Shrewsbury (*c.*1522–1590)', *Oxford Dictionary of National Biography*, Oxford University Press, 2004, online edn, May 20, [http://www.oxforddnb.com/view/article/26928]. Goldring states that the marriage of Bess and George Talbot took place in London on the 1st of November 1567, over three months *before* the marriages of the children. David Durant concludes his discussion of potential dates by stating "It is certainly safe to say that Bess and the Earl were married in the autumn of 1567...." Durant. D.N., *Bess of Hardwick: Portrait of an Elizabethan Dynast*, (1977), 55-56. Mary Lovell argues that the marriage of Bess and Talbot took place *after* the marriages of the children sometime between the 9th of February and the 23rd of March 1568, at a place unknown. Lovell. M.S., *Bess of Hardwick, First Lady of Chatsworth*, (2006) 200.

[5] In strict heraldic terms, as shields would be held on the arm and, thus, viewed by the holder from behind, the male's arms are said to be on the dexter side [right] and the female to the sinister side, [left].

[6] Only one of the surviving four panels is dated.

[7] There is no actual evidence that Bess commissioned the table but the inclusion of the Hardwick and Cavendish arms to depict the marriage of Bess and that of her eldest son, together with the words "we stags exult to the divine" would suggest that it was commissioned, probably by Bess, to celebrate the success of the Cavendish family whose coat of arms includes three stags therefore making it perhaps less likely that the table was commissioned by Talbot.

5

Matters of Birth and Death

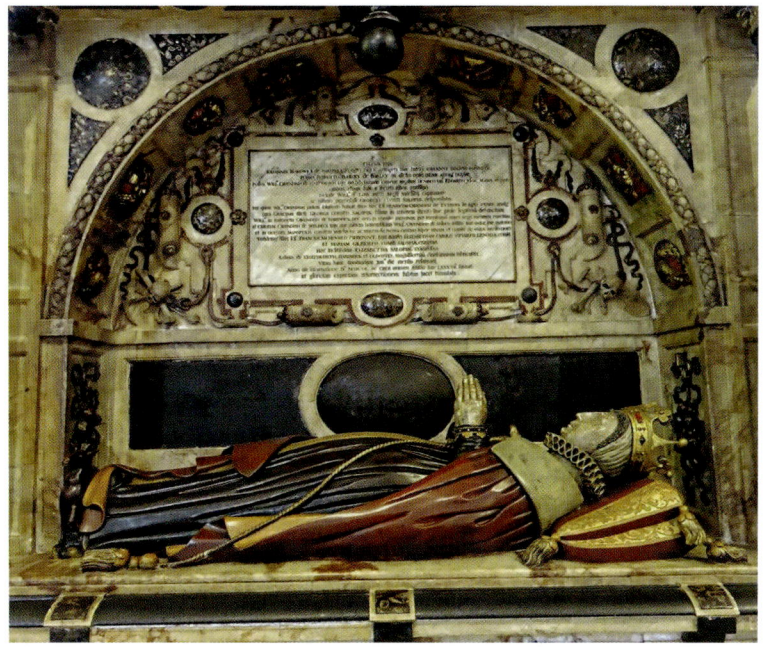

Bess's tomb, Derby Cathedral

MATTERS OF BIRTH .....

Recent biographers have begun to argue that Bess's year of birth was 1527. This would seem to have more to do with a desire to have her moving into Hardwick New Hall on her alleged seventieth birthday than it has to do with any credible historical evidence. Although an entry in the Hardwick household accounts for the 4th of October 1597 records a payment of 20s. to three of Bess's servants who played music when she moved into the new hall, there is no mention of the occasion having been her birthday, seventieth or otherwise.[1]

In his *Barlow Family Records*, Sir Montague Barlow claimed that Bess was 25 when she married Robert Barley, he does not provide any evidence to support his asertion.[2] If Bess had been 25 in 1543 then she would have to have been born in 1518. Robert Barley's date of birth is given as 10 December 1529 which agrees more or less with other evidence of his birth. Arthur Collins stated that Bess was 14 in 1543 when she married Robert Barley but for that to be so she would have to have been born in 1529, that is at least a year after her father's death.[3] Collins may have confused marriage with espousal. Had Bess been 14 when she was espoused to Robert Barley in the mid-1530s then her birth year would have been 1521/22. From the late nineteenth-century until recently it was generally accepted that Bess was born in 1520.

The assertion that Bess was born in 1527 is predicated on the erroneous notion that for girls the age of 16 was the legal age of majority or coming of age. In fact, in the sixteenth century, 16 was not an age of rite of passage in either Common or Canon Law.[4] Bess's brother James was born in 1525 and entered into his inheritance when he came 'of age' in 1546, i.e., when he reached the age of 21. In their wills testators often bequeathed legacies and provisions to daughters until they reached a given age and similar arrangements appear in marriage contracts. However, it is important to recognise that this age could vary depending upon local tradition. For example, when Gabriel Marmion agreed to marry Anne Cooper he bound himself to pay certain sums of money to her daughters when they attained the age of 19 (see Chapter 6). However, for common law purposes in the sixteenth century the legal age of majority, the age at which men and women came of age, was 21.

In matters of litigation, a woman could not be a sole plaintiff at common law unless she was a spinster or widow and had reached the age of 21. An unmarried woman or widow, a *femme sole*, would be represented by her legal guardian until she reached the age of 21. If she did not have a guardian the courts were empowered to nominate one to act on her behalf. A married woman, or *femme covert*, would be represented by her husband. It was possible for a married woman over the age of 21 to be sole plaintiff in a Chancery legal case. Bess's mother was the sole plaintiff in her desertion proceedings against Ralph Leche. Generally, the equity courts tended to follow the same procedures as the common law courts but offered swifter and cheaper judgements based on common sense rather than legal precedence.

Robert Barley died in December 1544 and the following year Bess commenced proceedings for dower in the Court of Common Pleas against Peter Freschevile and his ward, Robert's younger brother and heir George Barley. As sole plaintiff in these proceedings she must have been at least 21 in 1545. Therefore, Bess cannot have been born any later than 1524 and this, of course, assumes she was not already over the age of 21 when she began her Common Pleas proceedings. In 1546, as sole plaintiff, Bess switched her claim for dower to the equity court of Chancery. In her initial complaint to that court she referred to George Barley as "being within the age of 21"[5] demonstrating once again that 21 was the age of maturity. After Bess's marriage to Sir William Cavendish, the standard practice of husbands being named as plaintiffs in their wife's legal proceedings was employed.[6]

The gentry families of north-east Derbyshire formed a distinct interconnected, inter-related and self-conscious social group. There were long established connections and relationships between families such as the Frescheviles, Foljambes, Chaworths, Leakes, Boswells, Barleys and Hardwicks. Bess's great, great-grandfather Roger Hardwick married Nichola Barley c.1450. Robert Barley's great-grandfather was married to Eleanor Freschevile and Robert's mother was Elizabeth, daughter of James Chaworth. Robert's sister, Dorothy, married George Foljambe. In 1507 a young John Hardwick, later to become Bess's father, was conveyed property in Heath and six messuages at Hardwick by Sir Henry Willoughby of Wollaton, Ralph Greenhalgh and John Freschevile, which they had held as feofees of Roger Hardwick.

The Hardwicks and the Frescheviles were not only close neighbours, they were close relatives and as such the Frescheviles would have been aware of the year of Bess's birth. Within a complex web of relationships Peter Freschevile, who claimed guardianship over Robert Barley, and Bess were second cousins. Freschevile's mother was the daughter of John Leake and Elizabeth Savage. Bess's mother was the daughter of Thomas Leake and Margaret Fox. John and Thomas were the sons of William Leake of Sutton and Katherine Chaworth.[7] Had Bess been under the age of 21 when she commenced legal proceedings for dower Freschevile could be expected to have lodged an objection to those proceedings on the grounds that she was within age (i.e., under 21) but no such objection appears to have been made. The record of Bess's proceedings for dower in the Court of Common Pleas is not extant. However, in her 1546 complaint to Chancery Bess informed the court that in order to obtain her dower she had been compelled to sue Freschevile in the Court of Common Pleas, proceedings she is known to have begun in that court on the 28 March 1545.[8] If Bess was the sole plaintiff in her proceedings in Common Pleas, as her initial complaint to Chancery indicates that she was, she must have already reached the age of majority by 1545 and therefore could not have been born any later than 1523/4.

In his will dated January 1528 Bess's father John Hardwick placed his children in the custody of their mother.[9] She was to receive 26s 8d (2 marks) annually to provide meat and drink for their daughters until each reached the age of 15. If the age of majority was 16 why would John Hardwick have only provided for his daughters until their 15th birthday ? Why not to their 16th ? Bess's mother went on to marry Ralph Leche. Canon Law held that whereas a boy had to be 14 years of age to give his consent to marriage, girls could give consent from the age of 12. Boys under 14 and girls below the age of 12 were held to be too young to consummate marriage.[10] We know that by 1536/7 Ralph had purchased Robert Barley's wardship and marriage from Arthur Barley. If Bess was around 15 years of age at that time her mother would have ceased to receive the funds to provide for Bess's upkeep. Under such circumstances it would have made perfect sense for Ralph to have been seeking to arrange Bess's marriage. It is probable that Bess and Robert Barley were espoused c.1536/7 with the marriage ceremony and possible consummation of the marriage taking place later, that is prior to or shortly after Arthur Barley's death in 1543.

Applying modern notions of family life to the sixteenth-century family can lead to confusion and misinterpretation. It has been assumed that Bess was residing with her mother and stepfather at Hardwick before her marriage to Robert Barley. However, Ralph seems to have been keen to avoid the expense of paying for the upkeep of his stepdaughters once the provisions in their father's will had lapsed. Before Jane Hardwick married Godfrey

Boswell in or around 1546 she had been in service to Lady Carew. This raises the intriguing possibility that Bess, and perhaps elder sister Alice, may also have been placed in service before their marriages. Jane and Mary were certainly residing at Hardwick in the early 1540s when they were visited there by John and Anne Wyke. By that date Alice was the wife of Francis Leche and there is no mention of Bess having been there.[11] Assuming Jane was born in 1526/7 she would have reached the age of 15 in 1541/2 and it may have been around this time she entered Lady Carew's service. Ralph Leche's financial problems led him to sell Robert Barley's wardship and marriage to Henry Marmion in 1537/8.[12] Could it be that Bess entered service in an aristocratic household at this time ? Of course, there is no evidence that Bess was in service before her marriage to Robert Barley but there is equally no evidence that she was not. Absence of evidence, as one of my university professors used to say, is not evidence of absence.

There is no issue when it comes to the year John Hardwick's son James was born. As we have seen, James came out of wardship in 1546 so we can be certain that he was born in 1525. However, establishing the order of the births of John's daughters is more problematic. In a Chancery case begun c.1546/7 Jane Hardwick's husband Godfrey Boswell listed John Hardwick's daughters as Mary, Elizabeth, Alice, Dorothy and Jane.[13] He was suing for an unpaid marriage portion and most likely named his wife last as she was the object of his proceedings. The published version of the 1569 herald's visitation of Derbyshire lists Hardwick's daughters as Jane, Mary, Elizabeth and Alice. [14] Dorothy, possibly born at some time between 1518 and 1521, is not mentioned in the visitations and probably died young. In an early written account, the daughters are listed as Alice, Elizabeth, Mary and Jane but in a 1615 copy of the 1569 visitation they are listed as Mary, Jane, Alice and Elizabeth. In the published version of the 1569 visitation Alice and Mary are placed before their brother, James, but in two manuscript copies of the visitation Elizabeth and Jane are placed before James. Both hand-written pedigrees pair Alice with Elizabeth and Mary with Jane. Only the published version of the 1569 visitation pairs the daughters differently but this appears to be the result of the layout of the printed page. A manuscript pedigree dating from c.1565 would appear to list John Hardwick's children in reverse order commencing with Mary [not actually named but described as the wife of Wingfield] followed by Jane, James, Elizabeth and 'Anna' (that is Alice)[15]

Here again Mary is paired with Jane and Elizabeth with Alice. The most likely birth order of John Hardwick's daughters was Alice, Dorothy, Elizabeth, Jane and Mary. In the early 1540s Jane and Mary are the only two of Hardwick's daughters known to have been living at Hardwick.[16]

Hand-written Leake pedigree, c 1565, Belvoir Castle MSS

Ralph Leche married John Hardwick's widow around 1529. Alice, the eldest of John Hardwick's daughters, appears to have been the first to marry. Her ill-fated marriage to Francis Leche, her stepfather's nephew, may have been contracted sometime around her 15th birthday c.1533, which incidentally would have coincided with John Bugby's eviction from Hardwick. Francis was born on 1 November 1525 and would not have reached the age of 14 until 1539. Bess is believed to have married Robert Barley in May 1543 and Jane's marriage to Boswell appears to have taken place in 1545/6. In each case, espousals may have been contracted well before the marriages took place. Mary was quite possibly the youngest of Hardwick's daughters. Her marriage to Richard Wingfield appears to have been brokered by Sir William Cavendish and she was the only one of Hardwick's daughters not to marry into a local gentry family.

Although Bess had proved her fecundity during her marriage to Sir William Cavendish, it is possible that at the time of her marriage to Sir William St Loe she was close to the end of her child-bearing years. She would have been around 38 years of age at the time of the St Loe marriage and approaching her mid-40s at the time of St Loe's death. Women in the sixteenth century could have children well into their 30s. For example, Edward Seymour's second wife Anne Stanhope bore eleven children the last of which was born when she was 39/40. However, her first child was born when she was 16. Bess was around 27 when her first child Frances was born in 1548 by which time her child-bearing years would have been well advanced. St Loe had no issue from his first marriage and did not remarry for some 10 years after his first wife's death. He cannot have been anxious to produce a male heir.[17] The manner in which their marriage came about and the general lack of physical contact between them may indicate that St Loe was impotent.

The plaque on Bess's monument in Derby Cathedral states that she was around 87 when she died on 13 February 1608. Some object that the information on the plaque cannot be trusted because it refers to her grandson as 'Duke of Newcastle' which he did not become until 1655, 47 years after her death. However, all this shows is that a new plaque probably replaced an original one. The information regarding Bess's age at death given on the new plaque would simply have been copied from the original. The Duchess of Newcastle stated that Robert Barley and Bess were very young Robert when they married adding that he had died before the marriage had been consummated. However, she said this in 1667, over 120 years after the event and was simply attempting to make sense of what little was actually known at that time. According to law when a couple were espoused, unless coercion had been used, they were deemed to be married. However, the marriage contract was not complete until the marriage ceremony had taken place and the marriage consummated. Bess and Robert may well have been quite young when they were espoused. Such espousals often involved two people whose ages were many years apart. It cannot be assumed that the marriage ceremony of Robert and Bess took place at the same time as the espousal. We do not know for certain when the marriage ceremony took place. Bess informed Chancery that both she and Robert were of "tender years" when the marriage contract was agreed between Arthur Barley and Ralph Leche.[18] This suggests that the espousal was contracted sometime before any marriage ceremony took place. It is possible that Robert and Bess's marriage ceremony took place shortly after Arthur Barley's death prior to Robert's removal from Barley Lees. The marriage is *assumed* to have taken place shortly before the death of Arthur Barley on 28th May 1543 because when Godfrey Boswell purchased Robert's wardship from the crown apparently as an afterthought a note was added to the record stating that Robert was married in the lifetime of his father. To what extent this can be taken as reliable evidence of the timing of Bess marriage to Robert is open to question simply because in order to limit the impact of wardship on Arthur Barley's estate it was in Boswell's interest to have it recorded that Robert married before his father died. Bess's marriage to Robert lasted around 17 months. We do not know if the marriage was consummated, we do know that it produced no issue.

MATTERS OF DEATH .....

The August 2018 edition of the BBC's History magazine included Tracy Borman's article, *Schemer, Social Climber…Scourge of Elizabeth I* in which Dr Borman informs her readers that following her death in 1608 Bess's 'body lay in great state at Hardwick until her funeral three months later.'[19] I recall being told the same thing by a long time Hardwick room guide when I began my stint as a National Trust volunteer. Repeated *ad nausem*, it is utter nonsense !

It was long said that Mary, Queen of Scots, was at some time held in captivity at Hardwick. Of course, this myth has thankfully been consigned to the proverbial dustbin. However, many other myths persist. Bess did not meet her first husband in London and beyond speculation there is no hard evidence to show she was ever in service to the Zouches of Codnor or the Greys of Bradgate. It really does not help matters when "celebrity historians" presenting material to the wider public on TV, radio, or in popular publications repeat these myths as present them as facts. Of course, we may not know that some of the things we say are myths. Make no mistake, myths are hard enough to dislodge even where the evidence we have screams at us that something or other told time after time to visitors to such places as Hardwick are in fact myths. And the truth is that there are those among us, well-meaning souls no doubt, who are simply unwilling, or unable, to change their views even in the face of over-whelming evidence.

Let us now turn our attention to Bess's funeral. Bess died 13 February 1608. There are references in the Devonshire archives at Chatsworth House that indicate Bess's funeral took place on either the 16th or 17th of February together with an entry for February 1608 which states that the sum of £1 was distributed among the poor at the gates of Hardwick the day her corpse was transported to Derby.[20] In his unpublished 1692 manuscript *Lives of the Earls of Shrewsbury* Nathaniel Johnson wrote:

'The Lord Cavendish, Mr William, his sister; my self, John Clay, John Needham, & all the women but Mrs. Digby, And Cartwright, & all the men of note but Pudsey, attended the Corps to Derby on Tuesday, Multitudes came in to behold our coming. The baylives stept with us, & presented wine & two suger loaves to his Lordshipp ---- ffebruary ye: 18th...' [21]

We know that members of Bess's family stayed in two inns at this time, The George and The Talbot. Johnson's description fits well with Bess's own wishes for her funeral as expressed in her will. She asked to be buried without pomp and ceremony and typically without unnecessary expense.[22] Perhaps the definitive evidence in this case comes from Bess's contemporary Arthur Mower (1555-1610), a yeoman servant of the Barleys, who wrote:

'The old Countess of Shrewsbury departed forth of this world the Saturday being the 13th day of February at Hardwick and was carried to Derby of Tuesday the next after to her tomb there in All Hallows Church and there buried...' [23]

In her 2018 *Devices & Desires*, author Kate Hubbard makes some effort to incorporate recent research but nevertheless repeats the myth that Bess's funeral took place in May 1608.[24] Bess's funeral took place on Tuesday the 16th of February 1608. Her body did not lie in state at Hardwick for three months. So how did that myth come about? Records at Chatsworth refer to a funeral banquet held in May 1608.[25] This is likely to have been what we today would call a memorial service which was held in the more clement Spring weather of May when travel would have been far easier than in the cold, frosty weather of a Derbyshire winter. Misinterpreted as the date of Bess's funeral, it was the memorial service and banquet of May 1608 that gave rise to the myth that her corpse lay it state for three months in the High Great Chamber of Hardwick New Hall.

We do not have any documentary evidence that confirms Bess's date of birth. Parish registers were not introduced until 1538 and very few parishes have complete records from thence forward. There is no mention of a birthday in any of Bess's letters, sent or received. The weight of the evidence we do have indicates that the year of Bess's birth was 1521/22. Those authors who argue that Bess was born in 1527 do so on flimsy grounds. Equally misleading are claims that after her death Bess's corpse lay in state for three months in Hardwick Hall's High Great Chamber. The evidence provided by Nathaniel Johnson coupled with that of Arthur Mower is clear and unequivocal. Bess's funeral took place in Derby on Tuesday 16 February 1608.

REFERENCES & NOTES:

[1] Devonshire MSS, Chatsworth, Hardwick MSS 7, Account Book of Countess of Shrewsbury, 1591-97, fol. 195; M. Girouard, *Robert Smythson and the Architecture of the Elizabethan Era*, London, 196, 120.

[2] M. Barlow, *Barlow Family Records*, (London) 1932, 23. Interestingly, the author indicates his belief that Bess was older that James, pedigree, p 143.

[3] A. Collins, *Historical Collections of the Noble Families of Cavendishe, Holles, Vere, Harley and Ogle*, (London: Printed for E. Withers, 1752), 18.

[4] In sixteenth century law age of majority was 21 for males and females. The first time the age of 16 took on any legal significance was in 1929 when the Age of Marriage Act raised the age at which boys and girls could marry with the consent of parent or guardian from 14 to 16. This remains the case today. Until 1753 a marriage ceremony could take place anywhere providing it was conducted by an ordained minister and independently witnessed. The custom was that consummation of a marriage took place after any reception often in the early hours of the morning and was witnessed by friends and relatives. The 1933 Children and Young Persons Act made it illegal for those under the age of 16 to buy tobacco and cigarettes. This was in raised to 18 in 2015. Until 1970, the age at which men and women could vote was 21. Since 2003 codified laws allow those 18 and over to buy alcohol. However, harping back to the time when 21 was deemed the minimum age for buying alcohol many retailers ask for proof of age where customers look to be under 21 (or in some cases even under 25). Even today, although it is legal for those over 18 to buy alcoholic drinks, many supermarket and off-licence chains display Challenge 21 (or Challenge 25) notices stating that they will not serve people who look to be under 21 (or 25) without ID. In the USA the majority of states still use 21 as the minimum legal age for the consumption of alcohol.

[5] TNA, C 1/1101/17.

[6] TNA, C 1/1101/17; TNA, C 1/1120/44. For women and the law in the sixteenth century see A. Flower, *Tudor Women's Legal Rights, 1485-1603*, (2007).

[7] 'Pedigree of the Freschevile and Musard Families', *Collectanea Topographica et Genealogica*, (1837), 4.

[8] P. Riden. 'The Hardwicks of Hardwick Hall in the Fifteenth and Sixteenth Centuries', *Derbyshire Archaeological Journal*, 130 (2010), 151.

[9] TNA, E 150/743/8.

[10] Flower, 23. A marriage between a girl of 12 and a boy over 14 could be dissolved if it had not been consummated. Failure to consummate a marriage could and did result in child marriages being dissolved.

[11] TNA, STAC 2/17/53; TNA, STAC 2/22/240. See also chapter 6.

[12] C 1/860/14. See also chapter 2.

[13] TNA, C 1/1102/37-39.

[14] W.C. Metcalfe, (ed), *The Visitations of Derbyshire, 1569 and 1611*, Vol 7, 1891, 142; Riden. 'The Hardwicks', 150.

[15] Belvoir Castle Muniments, box labelled 'pedigrees'.

[16] TNA, STAC 2/17/53; TNA, STAC 2/7, ff 15-16.

[17] See chapter 2.

[18] TNA, C 1/1101/17.

[19] Borman. T., 'Schemer, Social Climber … Scourge of Elizabeth I', *BBC History Magazine*, August 2018, 50-55.

[20] Devonshire MSS, Chatsworth, Hardwick MS 29, 4.

[21] Nathaniel Johnson, *Lives of the Earls of Shrewsbury*, unpublished MS Chatsworth, 397-8.

[22] TNA, PROB 11/111/213.

[23] 'The Memorandum of Arthur Mower', *Barlow Family Records*, Chapter 3, 24.

[24] Hubbard. K., *Devices & Desires: Bess of Hardwick and the Building of Elizabethan England*, (London, Chatto & Windus), 2018, 296-97.

[25] Devonshire MSS., Chatsworth, Hardwick MS 29, 16.

Erratum:
P100 and p114, n.87
Henry Marmion died 4 Jan 1555, not 1554

6

The Marmion Connection

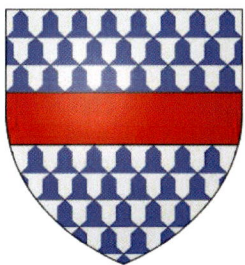

Arms of Marmion of Tamworth, Winteringham and Torrington

If students of Bess of Hardwick have come across any member of the Marmion family it will most likely have been Henry Marmion who, together with John Leake, was an executor of the last will and testament of Bess's father, John Hardwick. Although he features on numerous occasions in the Hardwick narrative, little is known about Henry and even less about his son Gabriel, grandson Francis and the so far unidentified Marmion whom Bess's fourth husband, George Talbot, Earl of Shrewsbury, bore animosity towards and described as his enemy and as Bess's 'right-hand man'.

The Marmions of Nottinghamshire were a cadet branch of an illustrious medieval family which can be traced from Robert son of Roger Marmion, who in the early twelfth century held lands in Lincolnshire and in Warwickshire near Tamworth (Staffs.).[1] The family is first found at Fontenay-le-Marmion (Calvados), about six miles south of Caen, in the mid-eleventh century. Robert died in 1144[2] and was succeeded by a son (d. c.1181), grandson (a prominent justice who died c.1216–18)[3] and great-grandson of the same name. The last Robert died probably c.1241–3. His son and heir, Philip, whose estates included the manor of Middleton (Warw.), later held by the Willoughbys, died in 1291, leaving three daughters and an illegitimate son. The family's estates passed to William

Marmion, the son and heir of Robert, the son of the justice. William appears to have been dead by 1276. His son and heir, Sir John Marmion, was summoned to Parliament between 1313 and 1322, thus becoming the 1st Lord Marmion. He died probably early in 1322, leaving a son and heir John, 2nd Lord Marmion, who is said to have died in 1335. His son and heir Robert was never summoned to Parliament and died without surviving male issue c.1360, when the barony, according to modern doctrine, fell into abeyance between his two sisters and coheirs. According to the nineteenth-century chronicler of the family, the Rippingale (Lincs.) branch of the Marmion family were descended from a younger son of the early thirteenth-century justice.[4] By the second half of the fifteen century the Rippingale Marmions were headed by Henry Marmion's uncle, Mauncer Marmion, (d 1506).

Henry Marmion was the eldest son and heir of another John Marmion (d. 1521). Alice, Henry's mother, was a daughter of Sir Hugh Willoughby (d. 1448).[5] John and Alice had another son named Francis and a daughter, Elizabeth. Possibly named for Sir Henry Willoughby (d. 1528), Henry Marmion was most likely born at Wollaton around 1495 and was a contemporary of Bess's father. On entering his inheritance in 1515/16 he commenced court proceedings to secure the repayment of a loan made by his father John to Thomas Dixon, parson of Rippingale.[6] In April 1545 Henry appointed John Burton as his attorney in a legal case in Bourne, also in south Lincolnshire, in relation to the surrender to George Machell, a relative of the Marmions, of a property formerly belonging to the monastery at Bourne.[7] At some date before 1547 Marmion was among several men accused of forcibly resisting an attempted arrest of Machell at Rippingale.[8] Among the defendants were Edith Marmion (d. 1538) of Lincolnshire, widow, and her son Edward. Edith was the daughter of Sir Thomas Berkley of Wymondham, Norfolk,[9] and the wife of Mauncer Marmion. They had three sons, Edward, William and Thomas, and a daughter, Petronell, who together with Henry Marmion was an executrix of her mother's will of 1539.[10] Edward went on to become the parson of St Botolph's, Billingsgate, in London. In his will, dated 23 September 1540,[11] he referred to his sister Petronell and to his cousin Henry Marmion's two daughters, Bridget and Ursula. Mauncer held the family estates, which suggests that Henry's father, John, was a younger brother. Mauncer's will, dated 8 November 1505, tells

The Marmion Connection

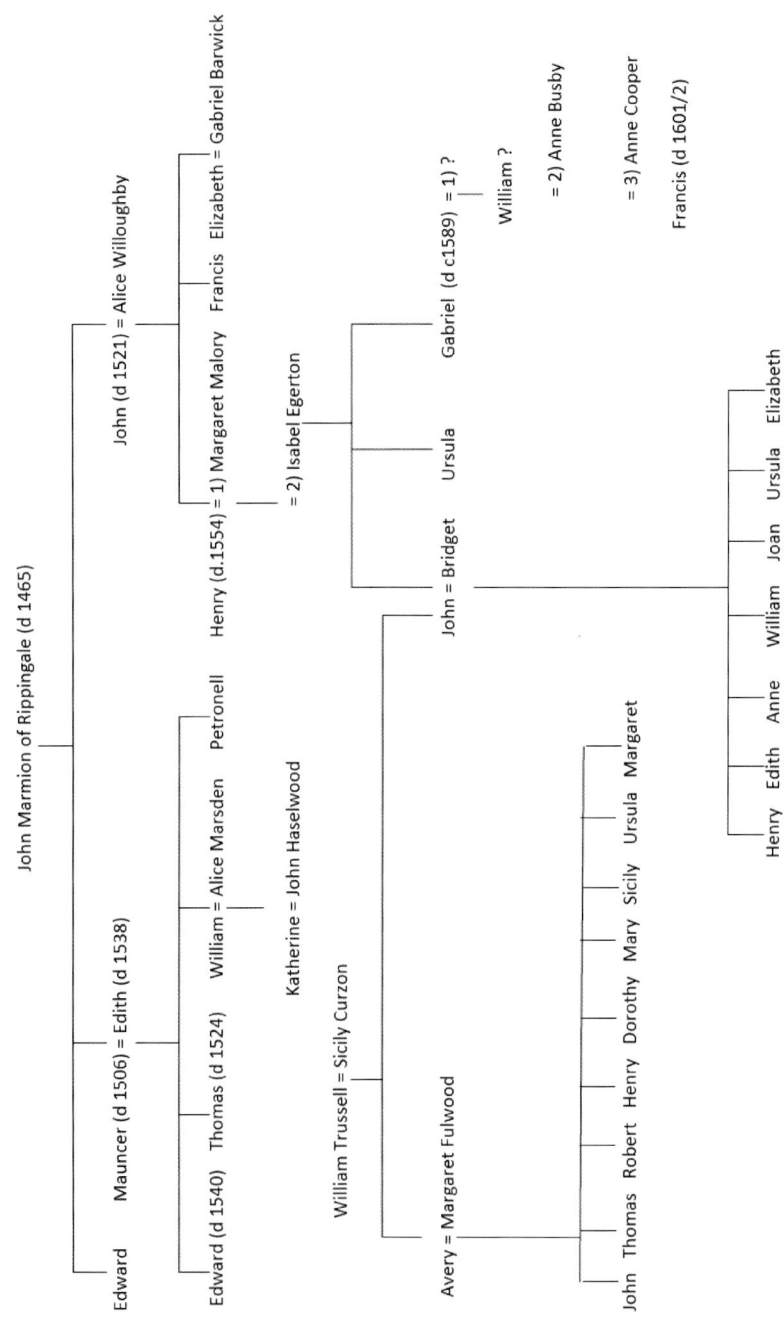

Marmion Pedigree

us that their father was another John Marmion and that their Lincolnshire ancestors were laid to rest in St Anne's chapel in the church of St Andrew at Rippingale.[12] The executors of Mauncer's will were his wife Edith and Sir Henry Willoughby.

In January 1519 John Willoughby and John Marmion presented Thomas Marmion (d. 1529/30)[13] as the new rector of the parish church of Dowesby (Lincs.)[14] William Marmion (d. 1520/1)[15] married Alice, the widow of John Marsden, and died sometime between 1515 and 1518. Alice was evicted from the farm she and William had shared at Ringsdon (Lincs), She commenced proceedings in Chancery against the two executors of William's will, his mother Edith and his brother Edward. Alice revived these proceedings after Edith's death in 1538. On this occasion the defendants were Petronell and Henry Marmion.[16] Katherine, William Marmion's heir, became a king's ward. She married John Haslewood (d. 1550) of Maidwell, Northamptonshire, who was master of the Fleet prison between 1548 and 50.[17] They commenced proceedings in Chancery against her grandmother Edith and her uncle Edward in relation to several manors in Lincolnshire and Leicestershire, which were part of her late grandfather Mauncer's estate.[18] In April 1535 a writ of Oyer and Terminer was issued by the Kesteven JP Thomas Gildon relating to an alleged assault on Haselwood by Henry Marmion.[19] It was probably during this affray that the attempt to arrest Machell had been made. Haselwood and his wife brought further complaints before Star Chamber alleging that Katherine had not received her dower or dues from her father's estate. Among the defendants were Edith, Edward, Machell and Henry Marmion.[20]

In June 1508 John Marmion was an executor of the will of Sir Henry Willoughby. By 30 October 1509 a marriage had been agreed between John Marmion and John Malory of Walton on the Wolds in Leicestershire in which Henry was to marry Malory's daughter Margaret.[21] As part of this agreement Margaret's marriage portion of land and tenements to an annual value of £10 at Walton and Croxton, also in Leicestershire, were enfeoffed to the use to of Henry and Margaret and their heirs. The feoffees were Sir Henry Willoughby, Sir Ralph Shirley, Sir John Digby, John Willoughby, William Wymesold, and Robert Peret (or Perrot), chaplain of Wollaton. The marriage settlement illustrates how such arrangements were business transactions. If Henry was to die before the marriage was consummated Margaret was to marry his brother Francis. Should Margaret die first Henry, on the advice of his father, was to marry another of John Malory's daughters. Should any of the marriages prove childless the marriage portion was to pass to John Malory's heirs. In February 1546 the lands and tenements at Croxton and Walton were transferred to Henry and Margaret under the Statute of Uses. In his will, dated 11 September 1521, John Marmion bequeathed to Henry a bay colt and 40s.[22]

There were long-standing connections between the gentry families of north-east Derbyshire and the Willoughbys of Wollaton and Middleton. Sir Hugh Willoughby (d.1448) married Isabel Foljambe of Walton near Chesterfield. Their son Richard (d. 1471) married Anne Leake of Cotham and their grandson, Sir Henry (d. 1528) took as his first wife Robert Markham's daughter, Margaret (d. 1490). They were the parents of John, Edward, another Henry and several daughters.[23] In 1496 one of these daughters, Margaret Willoughby, married Sir John Zouche of Codnor. They were the parents of Sir George Zouche, who married Anne Gainsford. In 1500 Henry Willoughby was among a group of feoffees appointed by Sir John Zouche to hold Codnor and his other Derbyshire estates.[24] One of the executors of the will of Henry, Lord Grey of Codnor (d. 1525), was Bess's maternal grandfather Thomas Leake who, together with Roger Johnson, was seised of the manor and castle of Codnor at the time of Lord Grey's death.[25] Grey had promised to sell Codnor to the Crown, which then sold the estate to Sir John Zouche. John Leake, Bess's great-uncle, can also be linked to the Zouches and Codnor Castle. In the early 1540s Sir George Zouche and his wife took seisin of Codnor Castle. Edward Willoughby married Anne, the daughter of Sir William Filliol of Woodlands, Dorset, whose sister Catherine (d. 1535) was married to Edward Seymour, the Lord Protector, and was the mother of John and Edward Seymour. They remained loyal to their father despite being disinherited by him. Edward spent part of 1551 in the Tower of London and his brother John died a prisoner there in 1552.[26]

In 1489, 1495 and 1507 Sir Henry Willoughby was among the feoffees chosen by members of the Hardwick family to hold lands on their behalf.[27] In 1528 Bess's father made his will and enfeoffed his estate to Sir

Henry Willoughby's son Edward, John Leake, Thomas Leake, Edward Beresford, Richard Spalton, Robert Peret and Henry Marmion.[28] Henry was a servant of the Willoughbys. Like his father he was a bailiff and collector.[29] We know that at one stage he lived at Aspley Hall in Radford (Notts.),[30] a property held by Lenton priory until it passed to the Willoughbys after the

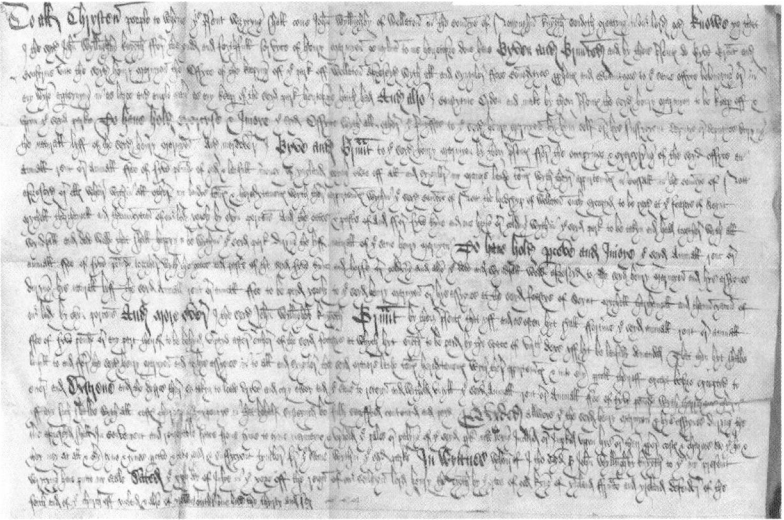

Sir John Willoughby's grant to Henry Marmion, 1544. (Crown Copyright)

dissolution of the monasteries. It was Sir Francis Willoughby's temporary home during the building of Wollaton Hall. In 1536 Henry acquired a twenty-year lease of a cottage and land at Basford (Notts.) from Hugh Willoughby of Maxstoke, Warwickshire.[31] In July 1544 Henry leased a messuage he was occupying in Cossall from Sir John Willoughby for 21 years at an annual rent of 40s. 10d.[32] In February 1523 Sir Henry Willoughby paid Henry Marmion 20s. in relation to correspondence and money sent to Edward Willoughby in London and in November an unnamed servant of Marmion was paid 1s. for the delivery of a letter.[33] Sir Henry died in 1528 and we learn from his will that Marmion had become one of two bailiffs of Wollaton Park. His duties included the 'keepership and payling and reconyng of Coles',[34] i.e. he had responsibility for maintaining the park pale and assessing royalties on coal. Several accounts in the Willoughby papers refer to Henry as bailiff of coal pits at Wollaton, Middleton, Sutton

Passeys, Gedling, Carlton, Trowell, Cossall and elsewhere including pits in Warwickshire and Leicestershire.[35] Those for 1544-5 inform us that Henry's annual fee was £5, making him one of the Willoughbys's highest paid servants.[36]

In July 1544, just five months before the death of Bess's first husband, Sir John Willoughby appointed Henry Marmion keeper of Wollaton park for life with an annual fee of £5, a gated pasture within the park for a horse or five cows, and the right to collect wood and windfall. Henry's fee was to be paid from the profits of Cossall and all Sir John's other manors in Nottinghamshire, excluding Wollaton. Should the fee not be paid for any reason Henry was entitled to distrain goods from those lands. At his own cost he was to provide good quality timber for repairing the park pale. [37] In September 1545 Henry's tenure of the keepership of Wollaton park was confirmed by Sir Henry Willoughby.[38] On 1 March 1548 Henry sold a capital messuage known as Le Ram situated in High Pavement,[39] Nottingham, which comprised a garden, outbuildings and taverns above and below ground to Joanna Hampton, her heirs and assigns. Sir Henry's will of 1549 referred to Henry as his 'trusty servant'.[40] Like Willoughby's other servants Marmion was often on the move, travelling from Wollaton to the sites of other Willoughby coalpits, as well as occasional journeys further afield to Bradgate, near Leicester, London and elsewhere.[41]

Sir Edward and Anne Filliol were the parents of another Sir Henry Willoughby, who inherited the estates of Wollaton and Middleton in January 1549 but was killed in Norfolk supressing the Kett Rebellion in August that year.[42] His wife was Anne Grey (d. 1548), daughter of Thomas Grey, marquis of Dorset, and sister of Henry Grey of Bradgate. Sir Henry Willoughby's untimely death in the summer of 1549 led to his young sons, Thomas and Francis, and their sister Margaret, first cousins to Henry Grey's daughters Jane, Katherine and Mary, being placed in wardship, initially with their uncle at Bradgate. Shortly afterwards Francis and Margaret became the wards of another uncle, George Medley (d.1562/3) of Titley, Essex, half-brother of Anne Willoughby and brother-in-law of both Henry Grey and Sir Henry Willoughby. As one of Sir Henry's 'three trusty servants' Medley joined Henry Marmion and Gabriel Barwick as witnesses of Sir Henry's will. As guardians of Sir Henry's children, they blocked a proposed marriage between Francis and Sir Francis Knollys's daughter, Elizabeth.[43] Medley had a house at the Minories in London, roughly midway between Aldgate and the Tower of London, where they were visited by Lady Grey and her daughters. Medley was placed in the Tower in the wake of the Jane Grey affair and once again at the time of the Wyatt rebellion, when the Minories was searched for incriminating evidence. Thereafter, Lady Grey met the costs of Francis's upkeep and education while Margaret was moved back to Bradgate. Thomas Willoughby had initially remained at Bradgate but was moved to London where he became the ward of Sir William Paget and married Dorothy, one of Paget's daughters. Thomas died in 1559, leaving his younger brother Francis as heir to the Wollaton and Middleton estates, of which he entered into possession in 1564.[44] There is ample evidence to demonstrate that the Greys, the Willoughbys and servants of both families regularly travelled between Wollaton and Bradgate.[45] Bess was always on good terms with Sir Francis Willoughby and several of her letters to him survive.[46] She paid visits to Wollaton and provided substantial loans and mortgages for Sir Francis's use. She also made good use of Sir Francis's servants, including his surveyor, Robert Smythson, the architect of Hardwick New Hall, and his master masons John and Christopher Rhodes and Thomas Accres, who had previously worked for Bess before being employed at Wollaton. They returned to her employment in August 1594.[47]

According to her husband Godfrey Boswell, John Hardwick's daughter Jane was at some point in service with Lady Carew [48] the wife of Sir George Carew. As captain of the ill-fated *Mary Rose,* Carew went to his death on 19 July 1545. Carew's first wife Thomasine (d. 1539/40) was the daughter of Sir Lewis Pollard. Her brother, Sir Richard, was in service with Sir William Courtney, during which time he came to the notice of Thomas Cromwell, and, like Sir William Cavendish, between 1537 and 1539 was involved in the suppression of the monasteries.[49] In the autumn of 1540 Sir George Carew married as his second wife Mary, daughter of Sir Henry Norris, and it is this Lady Carew whose household Jane Hardwick would have joined. Jane's service with Lady Carew would have ceased on her marriage to Boswell.

Clear links can be demonstrated between the Willoughbys of Wollaton, the Zouches of Codnor, the Greys of Bradgate and numerous others. Among these were the Hardwicks. It seems probable that Henry Marmion and John Hardwick knew each other before Henry was named a feoffee in 1528. Hardwick named Francis Talbot, 5th earl of Shrewsbury, and Sir John Savage as supervisors of his will and John Leake (d. 1545) and Henry Marmion as executors. Leake was his wife's uncle and the Leakes were also related to the Savages by marriage. Like his father, John Hardwick held land of both the Savage and Leake families.[50] The choice of Marmion may have been the result of Willoughby influence but may also indicate that a good degree of trust already existed between John Hardwick and Henry Marmion. John gave custody of his daughters to his wife until they reached the age of fifteen. Each daughter was left a marriage portion of 40 marks (£26 6s. 8d.) and was to adhere to the counsel of his executors.[51] Marmion and John Leake were to be the guardians of Hardwick's children.

John Hardwick's only son and heir James was within age at the time of his father's death and therefore subject to wardship. In March 1530 the Court of Wards sold James's wardship for £20 to a courtier named John Bugby. Probably with a degree of exaggeration conventional in Star Chamber proceedings, in 1533 Bugby claimed to have been forcibly evicted from Hardwick Hall by a gang of men led by John Leake and Henry Marmion.[52] According to Bugby's complaint, Marmion, Leake, Robert Garard, Jasper Flower and others, including a widow named Elizabeth Williamson, attacked Hardwick Hall 'riotously and with force', smashed glass in the windows, broke into the house and threw Bugby out. The widow's role would presumably have been to bring succour and comfort to Elizabeth and her children living in the house at the time. Bugby referred to several 'high commandments under great penalties' that had been sent to those accused and had been ignored. Bugby asked that the accused be ordered to appear before Star Chamber. Bugby's allegations were answered by Marmion and Leake who, aware that the penalties for riotous behaviour were severe, denied the accusations that any riot had occurred or that force had been used. They argued that Bugby's allegations were false and that the evidence against them was insufficient. They requested that the case be transferred from Star Chamber to the common law courts, probably because they knew that local jurors were sufficiently in their pocket that they would find in their favour, regardless of the truth of the matter. Also, if the case was to go to a common law court, the verdict would be a simple win or lose, based on a far more rigid interpretation of the law than might be possible under equity in Star Chamber, and they presumably saw that as helpful to them.

Around 1540 Marmion was alleged to have organised an attack on Chatsworth for which he, Bess's mother and others were brought before the Derby assizes and were later investigated by Star Chamber.[53] John Wykes claimed that Roger Leche had enfeoffed lands at Chatsworth to the use of his wife Anne for her lifetime, with reversion to Roger's son Francis Leche after Anne's death. Wykes married Anne in 1536. Wykes alleged that around 6 o'clock on the morning of 2 August 1540 Henry Marmion, his servant Nicholas Waterhouse, Edmund Plattes, who was Jane Hardwick's servant, and John Wild, of Hardwick, yeoman, together with a dozen or more 'evil-disposed and riotous persons', launched an armed attack on Langley Close at Chatsworth, assaulted Anne Wykes and Mary Hone, and then drove off with three cartloads of wheat sheaves. When questioned by Star Chamber, Wild, Waterhouse and Plattes all denied charges of riotous or unlawful assembly, forcible entry, assault or battery and asked that the case be tried at common law.

The defendants also claimed that after Roger Leche died, Anne held the property for her life and married a George Findern, and that they leased Langley Close to Henry Marmion. Henry manured the land and sowed it with wheat. Before the wheat was ripe Findern died and Anne married John Wykes. Meanwhile, Henry Marmion sold the crops growing in Langley Close to Jane and Mary Hardwick. At harvest time Jane and Mary ordered John Wild and Edmund Plattes to cut the crops and Marmion instructed Waterhouse to deliver them to Hardwick which, they stated, they did in a peaceful manner. Wykes claimed that during the attack his wife's head was 'broken' and that one of the defendants left behind a wood-knife and other weapons. According to Wild, Henry Marmion, Elizabeth Hardwick, Edmund Plattes, Nicholas Waterhouse, Robert Simpson, Thomas Thorpe and Wild himself were indicted and brought before the justices at Derby. There the defendants repeated their claim that they had not behaved in a riotous manner and stated that as Marmion's lease to Langley Close had been granted by Findern it became void on his death. Realising this, Marmion had granted the crops growing on the land to Jane and Mary Hardwick, pretending it to be a sale. The defendants also claimed that

Wykes and Anne went to see Jane and Mary and offered to allow the crops to be taken on condition that the sisters acknowledged Anne Wyke's rights over the land. The sisters refused and arranged for the defendants to carry away the crops. Waterhouse accepted that the knife was his but denied that it been used for any violent purposes or that Anne Wykes's head had been 'broken'. They also denied that Henry Marmion had unlawfully granted the crops to the Hardwicks. Wild stated that several women armed with pikes and staves had attacked the defendants as they took away the crops. He admitted that he had hit Anne Wykes and Mary Hone with his gadd (a sharp, pointed stick) and stated that he was responsible for having 'broken' Anne Wykes's head but he only did so in self-defence. The defendants agreed that they had been paid for their services by Henry Marmion and Jane and Mary Hardwick.

Bess's stepfather Ralph Leche purchased the marriage and wardship of Robert Barley in the 1530s. No later than 1538, when Ralph was in the Fleet prison for debt and accused of desertion by Bess's mother, Henry Marmion claimed that he had purchased Robert's marriage and wardship from Ralph.[54] John Hardwick's will of 1528 provided money for his daughters' maintenance until they reached the age of fifteen. In Bess's case this meant that she would have been provided for by her father's will until 1536/7, which tallies with the period during which Ralph Leche purchased Robert Barley's wardship and marriage. In 1543/4 Peter Freschevile of Staveley began proceedings against Ralph, Bess's mother and Henry Marmion, alleging that they had forcibly abducted Robert Barley and that a supposed marriage at an unspecified date between Robert and Bess was illegal.[55] At the same time Robert Barley's mother commenced similar proceedings for dower in the Barley estate and Henry Marmion was again one the defendants.[56] In 1545, when seeking dower from George Barley and his guardian Peter Freschevile, Bess claimed that large sums of money had been paid for Robert's marriage and wardship by an unspecified number of friends but she did not say who these were or how much was paid.[57] She may have been referring to Ralph Leche's initial payment to Arthur Barley, Robert's father, Henry Marmion's payment of £41. 9s. 2d.[58] and the 100 marks paid by Godfrey Boswell to the Court of Wards in or around 1544.[59] Boswell married Bess's sister, Jane Hardwick, probably in 1545/6, which may indicate that Jane was younger than Bess. We know that Ralph Leche was then in the Fleet prison 'condemned in great sums of money'.[60] It was also at that time that Sir James Foljambe began legal proceedings against Ralph Leche 'late of London', Bess's mother Elizabeth Leche of Hardwick Hall, Godfrey Boswell and Joan his wife late of Hardwick Hall, and their servant Edmund Plattes, to recover a debt of 20 marks.[61] Henry Marmion was not involved in this case but in 1545/6 Boswell commenced a suit in Chancery against him and John Leake (and again in 1546/7 against John's son and heir, Francis) with respect to unpaid money owed to his wife.[62] Boswell claimed that Marmion, Leake and Ralph Leche had embezzled hundreds of pounds which, as John Hardwick's executors, Marmion and Leake should have paid to Hardwick's daughters. Boswell stated that when Jane had been in the service of Lady Carew, Marmion had given £15 for Jane's apparel to her mother but that nothing else had been paid to any of John Hardwick's daughters.[63]

Apart from this payment of £15 we know nothing of Jane Hardwick's service with Lady Carew or how such a placement came about. Having secured her marriage to Godfrey Boswell it seems doubtful that a debt-ridden Ralph Leche would have wanted the financial burden of welcoming a 23-year-old newly widowed Bess back into the family after less than two years of marriage to Robert Barley. Bess was left to battle in the courts for her widow's dower and at one point in 1545 offered to settle the matter in return for her £26. 6s. 8d. marriage portion. It has often been claimed that around this time Bess entered the service of the Greys or the Zouches[64] but nothing is known of how such an arrangement might have come about. The Willoughbys were related to both the Greys and the Zouches. We have already seen that there is clear evidence linking the Leakes with the Zouches and it is possible that Bess may have been recommended to the Zouches by the Leakes. Henry Marmion was a valued and trusted servant of the Willoughbys and the evidence we have demonstrates that Marmion did have a care for John Hardwick's children and generally adhered to the commitments placed on him by John's will.

Henry Marmion died at Wollaton on 4 January 1554, having been predeceased by his first wife Margaret. In August 1564 an inquest was held at Lutterworth, Leicestershire, to enquire into the lands and tenements in Croxton and Walton which Henry had received from John Malory at the time of his marriage to Malory's daughter Margaret.[65] The jury stated that Henry had died without 'heirs of his and Margaret's bodies.' In November 1522 accounts refer to a payment of 6s. 8d. made by Sir Henry Willoughby to Gabriel Barwick, who is described as the husband of Henry Marmion's sister Elizabeth.[66] In 1525 a half-year wage of 20s. each was paid to Henry Marmion and Barwick.[67] In June of that year Henry was one of three men chosen by Sir Henry Willoughby to act as feofees in relation to a messuage and lands in Bramcote belonging to Hugh Wright.[68] Three years later Gabriel, George Medley and John Hall were the executors of Sir Henry Willoughby's will.[69] In 1542 Marmion, Barwick and Barwick's servant were paid dinner expenses when they attended Nottingham assizes. Henry was paid his fee of £5 in 1546 whilst Gabriel received 53s. 4d.[70] In his will of 1548 Sir John Willoughby granted Gabriel an annuity of 26s. He also bequeathed £20 each to his sister Alice Draycott and her daughter, another Alice, with the proviso that should either or both die before the legacy was paid, the money of the deceased was to go to Henry Marmion and Barwick. Also mentioned in the will was a sum of £3 3s. which Marmion and Barwick were to hold jointly for a period of twenty years; £3 was to be dispersed among the poor and the remaining 3s. was to go to the residents of Willoughby's two Wollaton alms-houses. The rents of lands in Wigginton, near Tamworth, with a yearly value of 26s. 8d., were granted to Henry and Gabriel for twenty years, the income to be used to repair roads and bridges and at their discretion for any other charitable deeds.[71] Sir John named Barwick as an executor of his will and Henry Marmion was among the witnesses. Together with John Hall, Gabriel from time to time presided over the Willoughby's court baron at Cossall.[72] Gabriel Barwick made his will in February 1568 and left 40s. to his godson, Gabriel Marmion. Barwick died in 1570.[73]

Willoughby family papers refer to a Gabriel Marmion as having been among Sir Francis Willoughby's favourite servants.[74] Henry Marmion's inquisition states that his marriage to Margaret Malory was childless.[75] The 1569 heralds' visitation of Nottinghamshire indicates that Henry married again after Margaret's death.[76] His second wife was Isabel, daughter of John Egerton of Wrinehill, Staffordshire (d. 1529). Sir Henry Willoughby's third wife was Helen, Egerton's eldest daughter. Henry Marmion was, therefore, Sir Francis's brother-in-law.[77] As we have seen,

Edward Marmion's will states us that Henry had two daughters, Bridget and Ursula. The 1569 visitation lists Bridget, daughter of Henry Marmion, as the wife John Trussell gent. of Cossall and informs us that the couple named one of their daughters Ursula.[78] Trussell came from a Warwickshire family and by the early 1540s was in service with the Willoughbys at Wollaton. Like Henry Marmion, he was a bailiff and collector and the two men are frequently paired together in the Willoughbys' accounts.[79] In 1568 Gabriel Barwick chose Trussell as an executor of his will.[80]

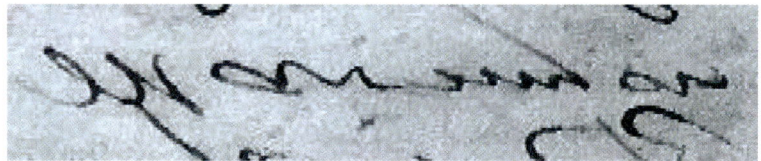

October 24, 1582/3: 'Marmyon': but which Marmyon ?

Although Edward Marmion's will refers only Henry Marmion's daughters it does not mean that Henry did not have a son (or sons) who may have been provided for outside the will.[81] Gabriel Marmion was almost certainly Henry's son, probably named for Gabriel Barwick. He emerges in the historical record in 1568 among the beneficiaries of Barwick's will and the following year he was one of the parties in a deed of sale.[82] In 1576, described as Bess's servant, Gabriel had the important job of being one of the witnesses to Bess and the earl of Shrewsbury's settlement relating to the estate of Sir William Cavendish.[83] In a letter to Bess dated 21 June 1580 the earl asked her to arrange for 'Marmyon' meet his son Gilbert at Bakewell but did not give this man's Christian name.[84] In a letter dated 24 October (the year is not given) to Sir Francis Willoughby the writer, 'Marmyon', described himself as a man the earl of Shrewsbury could not abide but again did not give his Christian name. He informed Sir Francis that he and Bess were blamed by Shrewsbury for the earl's loss of favour with Queen Elizabeth, of having spoken egregiously against him and of have been responsible for the queen's reduction in the allowance received by the earl for the Queen of Scots' diet. The writer also said that he knew he was hated by the earl on the grounds that he was his bitter enemy and Bess's 'right hand man'.[85] The allowance the earl received for the Scottish queen's diet was reduced on 29 January 1581 and she was removed from Shrewsbury's custody in August 1584. By 1583 Shrewsbury and Bess were no longer living as husband and wife and in July 1584 she was forced to leave Chatsworth.[86]

The writer of the letter to Sir Francis stated that he had been reluctant to leave Sir Francis Willoughby's household to serve Bess and was anxious to return saying 'Wollaton House should not be without a Marmyon', possibly a reference to the fact that the writer was aware that Gabriel Marmion was preparing to leave Wollaton. The identity of the writer is uncertain. From the 1550s entries in the Willoughby papers tend to refer to 'Marmyon' but, as with Shrewsbury's 1580 letter to Bess, the entries fail to provide a Christian name. It has been suggested that the writer was the William Marmion mentioned in the Willoughby accounts for 1572.[87] However, according to a Chancery deposition of 1602,[88] Gabriel had only one child, Francis, born c.1586, who was probably named for Sir Francis Willoughby. The fact that the writer mentions his father would seem to rule out William as having been the author. When he left her employ Bess provided the writer with an annuity of £40 which was to be paid out of the lands of her son William Cavendish. This encouraged him to hope that his unnamed father-in-law would be assured that he was able to support his wife, which in turn suggests that she may still have been living with her father.

The letter provides a significant clue to indicate that the author was the son of Gabriel Marmion when he writes that Bess was supporting his father's 'cause against Browne'.[89] The will of Thomas Busby of Mayfield, Staffordshire, refers to Gabriel Marmion as the testator's son-in-law.[90] It does not name Gabriel's wife, who is not mentioned in the will and may not have been alive when it was written. However, in 1602 she is identified as 'Anne Haste alias Harryson alias Busby',[91] Thomas Busby's 'base daughter'. Either she had two other husbands before Gabriel, or, far more likely, one (or both) of the other surnames refers to her mother (who may have been born Haste and married a Harrison, or vice versa). The 'alias Busby' presumably indicates that Thomas Busby acknowledged her as his daughter. The fact that she is not described as 'alias Marmion' is probably to avoid confusion with the defendant, but it is also possible that the will was drawn up after their betrothal and that Anne had died before or soon after her marriage to Gabriel. Thomas Busby's will may have been designed to reward Gabriel for marrying his illegitimate (but by 1577 deceased) daughter, or they were still married or about to be married. However, the will refers consistently to the 'heirs of Gabriel' pointedly not to Gabriel and Busby's daughter, which is unusual. Either this was a very deliberate sop to Gabriel, allowing his family to keep the money even if Anne died, or Anne had already died. Busby's wife Isabel was to enjoy the issues, revenues and profits of her husband's lands and farms in Mayfield and Burston in the manor of Stone, Staffordshire. These were to pass to Gabriel or his heir male on condition that within two months of Isabel's death he bound himself to pay £5 twice yearly to Busby's daughter Agnes, alias Harrison. Either the will was reflecting an unusually advantageous arrangement for Gabriel - something that a father would not normally have proposed for a legitimate daughter - possibly to induce him to marry an illegitimate daughter, or Anne Busby was dead when Busby made his will and Gabriel was being compensated for his loss. Should Gabriel die without a male heir this part of Isabel's legacy was to pass to William Browne, Mary his wife and their heirs male. Mary Browne was Isabel's daughter but is nowhere described as a daughter of Thomas Busby.

Busby's will was not proved until 1584, seven years after his death, and possibly due to the birth of Gabriel's son Francis in 1585/6 the dispute between Gabriel and Browne seems to have abated. It was to re-emerge after Gabriel's death when the date of his death and that of Francis appear to have been a central issue. Anne Busby may not have been Gabriel's first wife. William Marmion may have been Gabriel's son from an earlier marriage and died before his father. Gabriel's marriage to Anne Cooper could have been prompted by Gabriel's need for a male heir. Gabriel died intestate sometime between 1587 and 1589. In January 1590 Gabriel's widow Anne applied for a grant to administer her late husband's estate [92] and on 18 April 1594 Sir Francis Willoughby granted her a licence to alienate property in Arnold.[93] In April the following year she was conveyed a cottage and land in nearby Basford.[94]

In 1602 William Browne commenced proceedings in Chancery against Anne Marmion.[95] A writ dated 28 June 1602 called for depositions to be taken and these were presented to the court on 9 October. They provide a good deal of additional information which helps to clarify Brown's continuing grievances. Gabriel's wife Anne Cooper had provided him with a male heir, Francis, who died of smallpox in 1601/2 at the age of 16 years 10 months. According to the deposition made by Ralph Smith, Anne made Francis make a will leaving the income from the Busby lands and farms to her. Busby's will refers to another daughter, Agnes Busby alias Harrison. Rowland Harrison of Hassop, Derbyshire, probably a relative of Anne and Agnes Busby, stated in his deposition that Francis had made him sole executor of his will but he had refused and so administration was granted to Anne Marmion. This was confirmed by others including Anne's son Robert Cooper and Henry Watts of Aston near Stone (Staffs.) who had married Isabel Busby. Busby's will intended that, for the remaining term of his leases, the profits of his lands and farms in Mayfield and Burston were to go to his wife Isabel during her lifetime. After her death they were to pass to Gabriel and his heir male or, should that line die out, to William and Mary Browne. Isabel outlived Mary Browne, Gabriel and his son Francis but she herself was dead by June 1602. Anne Marmion had retained the profits from the Staffordshire lands and farms. By the terms of Busby's will, Francis should not have been able to grant the profits accruing from the lands and farms to his mother, even if his mother had been Busby's daughter.

A brief note to Sir Francis Willoughby dated 28 October was added to the margin of the letter of the 24 October in which the writer refers to having his own male servant. The writer must have travelled from Chatsworth to Sheffield between the 24 and 28 October when the letter was sent. Given Shrewsbury's animosity towards the writer, the fact that the letter, with the addition, was sent from Sheffield suggests that it was written before Bess was driven out of Chatsworth in July 1584. In other words, in October 1582 or 1583. Although there seems to be no firm evidence that William Marmion was a son of Gabriel it remains a possibility as the depositions of 1602 stating that Francis was Gabriel's only child may relate to a child then living or solely born to Anne Cooper and need not be conclusive evidence that Gabriel did not have a son with his other wives.

William may have been Gabriel's son and left Wollaton in 1572 to enter Bess's service. He may also have been the Marmion referred to in

Shrewsbury's letter of 1580. It is possible that William was the writer of the letter of 24 October. The letter was presumably despatched on or shortly after the addition was penned, i.e., 28 October 1582 or 1583. On leaving Bess's service the writer, armed with his £40 annuity, expressed a desire to enter the Inns of Court or seek a position with Lord Burghley or the earl of Leicester, saying that he would consult with his father and adhere to his counsel. This, together with the writer's need to impress his father-in-law, suggests that he was a relatively young man. If this really was William Marmion it would explain his absence from the Willoughby papers after 1572. No-one with the surname Marmion entered any of the Inns of Court between 1557 and 1597.[96] The Willoughby accounts record that in 1584 someone named Marmion gave £40 to the use of Sir Francis Willoughby,[97] the same sum as the annuity given by Bess to the writer of the 24 October letter and its addition, This Marmion may have been William, although at that time Gabriel was still in service with the family. The evidence we have suggests that the man involved in attempts to discredit Sir Francis Willoughby's wife Elizabeth Littleton during the 1570s and his son-in-law Sir Percival Willoughby in the 1580s was Gabriel. He had leased the manor house at Arnold from Sir Francis Willoughby in April 1584 around the time of his marriage to Anne Cooper and appears to have left Wollaton in 1585 and moved to the Arnold property with his new wife who was probably pregnant at the time. Gabriel wrote a letter to Sir Francis Willoughby from London in 1585 regarding Dorothy Willoughby's marriage to Henry Hastings which took place at Wollaton in 1587.[98]

Bess and the earl of Shrewsbury were not the only couple experiencing marital problems. In 1572 Sir John Littleton, father of Sir Francis Willoughby's wife Elizabeth, wrote to his son-in-law accusing 'Marmyon' of being a principal among those being encouraged by Sir Francis's sister, Margaret, Lady Arundel, to cause the breakdown of his daughter's marriage.[99] Avery Trussell's son John appears to have sided with Lady Willoughby and by referring to the Marmion involved as his 'uncle' makes it clear this was Gabriel.[100] In 1585 Sir Percival Willoughby's father claimed that Sir Francis did little without the counsel of a small clique of servants that included 'Marmyon'.[101] This date, which coincides with Gabriel leaving Wollaton, is the last sixteenth-century entry in the Willoughby papers relating a Marmion.

Gabriel was once more described as Bess's servant in his marriage settlement of June 1584.[102] Made between Gabriel on the one side and Adam Cooper, citizen and clothworker of London, and Robert Eyre of Blyth Spital (Notts,), the indenture records that Gabriel had agreed to marry Anne Cowper or Cooper, the widow of Robert Cooper, vintner, of St Mary's parish, Nottingham. One of the beneficiaries of Thomas Busby's will was Robert Quarnby of Nottingham, son of Humphrey Quarnby, alderman and three times mayor of the town.[103] The Willoughbys were related to the Thurlands, another of Nottingham's most influential families, who are mentioned several times in the Willoughby papers.[104] It is quite possible that Gabriel knew Robert Cooper. Robert was possibly the son of the Thomas Cooper who served as the mayor's sergeant in 1556-7 and the brother of Nottingham attorney, Thomas (alias Dennis) Cooper, who held the office of bailiff's sergeant in 1574 and sheriff's sergeant the following year.[105] Robert was town sheriff in 1571-2 and the following year would have been admitted to the Clothing.[106] He became a member of the corporation in 1577[107] and undertook military training in 1577 and 1578 with the town's trained bands.[108] Robert appears in a list of parishioners of St Mary's in 1582 which also includes a 'widow Cowper', who may have been either Robert's mother or the woman who two years later married Gabriel Marmion.[109] In 1584 Robert is recorded as not having attended the Clothing since 1582, quite probably the year he died.[110] In the marriage indenture Gabriel agreed to pay certain sums to Anne's seven children from her marriage to Robert. On reaching the age of 21 her two sons, Robert and Adam, were to receive £20 and £60 respectively. On attaining their nineteenth birthdays the five girls were each to be given £40.[111] In 1584 Anne's children were between the ages of two and sixteen, the eldest having been born in 1568. The couple made their home at a property in Arnold. In 1588, Gabriel may have been the 'Maister Marmeon' of whom Nottingham's Mickletorn Jury made complaint of his 'settting the town's ground to a farynar'.[112]

The connections between the Hardwicks, Leakes, Willoughbys and Marmions were important and help to shed further light on Bess's of Hardwick's life prior to her marriage in 1567 to George Talbot, Earl of Shrewsbury, of which less is known than of her later years. By the early 1540s her sister Jane had entered the service of the Carews but whether Bess entered the service of either the Zouches of Codnor or the Greys of Bradgate in or about 1545 or perhaps before is less clear. How the sisters came to be placed in such service is unknown but it may have been on the recommendation of the Leakes, the Willoughbys or Henry Marmion who, along with other members of his family, played a significant role in the affairs of the Hardwicks.

REFERENCES & NOTES

[1] Paragraph based, except as indicated, on the article on the medieval baronial family contributed by Sir Charles Clay to *Complete Peerage,* VIII, 505–22.

[2] P. Coss, Robert Marmion (d. 1144), *Oxford Dictionary of National Biography*, 2004, https://doi.org/10.1093/ref:odnb/18081

[3] H. Summerson, Robert Marmion (d. 1216-18), *Oxford DNB*, https://doi.org/10.1093/ref:odnb/18082

[4] C.F.R. Palmer, *History of the Baronial Family of Marmion* (Tamworth) 1875, , 117-19; Rev. S. Lodge, *Scrivelsby, The Home of Champions*, (London), 1894, 30-42.

[5] Willoughby family, *Oxford Dictionary of National Biography*; University of Nottingham Manuscripts and Special Collections, biog. note on Sir Hugh Willoughby; The Visitation of Nottinghamshire lists Henry as having married an unnamed sister of Robert Willoughby, Visits. Notts. 147. It is unclear if this is simply an error or evidence of a third wife.

[6] TNA, C 1/430/18; TNA, C 1/545/3

[7] Northamptonshire Archives, FH 1320.

[8] TNA, STAC 2/25/327-328; STAC 2/33/4; STAC 2/37/4.

[9] A. R. Maddison, *Lincolnshire Pedigrees* (1902), 127-8.

[10] TNA, C 1/852/27-31.

[11] TNA, PROB 11/28/534.

[12] TNA, PROB 11/15/39.

[13] TNA, REQ 2/6/212.

[14] UNMASC Mi 6/177/96.

[15] TNA, E 150/554/11, E 150/1127/8, C 142/35/31, C 142/37/86.

[16] TNA, C 1/852/21-26, C 1/852/27-31, C 1/861/28, C 1/852/21-26, C 1/861/28.

[17] F. Haselwood, *The Genealogy of the Family of Haselwood: Wickwarren, Belton and Maidwell Branches*, (1875), 2-3. John succeeded his father Edmund (d 1548) as Master of the Fleet Prison.

[18] TNA, C 1/519/55, C 1/427/25; C 1/546/53; C 1/849/9; C 1/861/28, C 1/852/21.

[19] Northamptonshire Archives, FH 1702.

[20] TNA, STAC 2/25/327-328; C 1/849/9; C 1/849/9-13; TNA, C 1/427/25; C 1/852/21; C 1/861/28.

[21] TNA, E 40/14639.

[22] Borthwick Institute for Archives, University of York, 17184384.

[23] UNMASC, biog. note on Sir Hugh Willoughby.

[24] TNA, E 40/10747; E 40/547.

[25] TNA, E 40/547.

[26] UNMASC, biog. note on Sir Henry Willoughby.

[27] P. Riden, 'The Hardwicks of Hardwick Hall in the Fifteenth and Sixteenth Centuries', *Derbyshire Archaeological Journal*, 130 (2010), 146-7.

[28] TNA, E 150/743/8.

[29] *HMC Middleton*, 307-8.

[30] TNA, STAC 2/17/53.

[31] TNA, STAC 2/17/53; C 146/7541; UNMASC Mi D 403.

[32] *HMC Middleton*, 338, 353.

[33] TNA, PROB 11/22/542.

[34] *HMC Middleton*, 314.

[35] ibid, 315.

[36] ibid, 317.

[37] UNMASC, Mi 6/175/46.

[38] J.W. Clay (ed.), *North Country Wills; being abstracts of wills relating to the counties of York, Nottingham, Northumberland, Cumberland, and Westmorland, at Somerset House and Lambeth Palace 1383 (1908), Wills proved in the Prerogative court of Canterbury*, 201; *HMC, Middleton*, 149. Henry Marmion was named as one of the supervisors of the 1551 will of John Barker of Radford, and as guardian of Barker's children. Clay, North Country Wills, 217-18; HMC Middleton, 338.

[39] UNMASC, Mi D 1633.

[40] UNMASC, Mi D 810.

[41] UNMASC, biog. note on Sir Henry Willoughby.

[42] J.G. Nichols (ed.), *The Chronicle of Queen Jane and Queen Mary* (Camden Society Old Series, 48, 1850), 66; *HMC Middleton*, 520, 396-97, 399, 400-3. Lady Grey and her three daughters visited Francis and Margaret Willoughby at Titley on the 24/25 October 1550, Mary Grey being described as 'deformed'.

[43] UNMASC, Mi 6/178/49.

[44] UNMASC, biog. note on Sir Francis Willoughby.

[45] e.g., *HMC Middleton*, 519.

[46] UNMASC Mi C23; UNMASC Mi 6/171/48; *HMC Middleton*, 161.

[47] D. N. Durant and P. Riden (eds), *The Building of Hardwick Hall, 'Part 2', The New Hall, 1591-98* (Derbyshire Record Society 9, 1984), p. xlix.

[48] TNA, C 1/1102/37/9.

⁴⁹ *History of Parliament, Commons 1509-58*, 122-3.

⁵⁰ TNA, C 142/21/35 in which John Hardwick, Bess's father, is stated as being eleven years old; E 150/743/8; C 142/73/27 (copy in Notts. Archives, DD/P/114/10).

⁵¹ TNA, E 150/743/8.

⁵² TNA, STAC 2/7, ff. 15-16.

⁵³ TNA, STAC 2/17/53.

⁵⁴ Riden, 'Hardwicks', 152: T. Kilburn, 'The Wardship and Marriage of Robert Barley: First Husband of Bess of Hardwick', DAJ, 134 (2014), 198.

⁵⁵ TNA, C 1/1101/17; Kilburn, 'Wardship' 197, 202.

⁵⁶ TNA, CP 40/1120.

⁵⁷ TNA, C 1/1102/17.

⁵⁸ Riden, 'Hardwicks', 152; Kilburn, 'Wardship', 198.

⁵⁹ ibid.

⁶⁰ TNA, C 1/1101/17.

⁶¹ TNA, C 1/1365/5-7.

⁶² TNA, C 1/102/57-59; C 1/1102/40-41.

⁶³ TNA, C 1/1102/37/9.

⁶⁴ D. N. Durant, *Bess of Hardwick: Portrait of an Elizabethan Dynast*, (2008), 12; M. S. Lovell, *Bess of Hardwick, First Lady of Chatsworth* (2005), 15-26; Riden, 'Hardwicks' 152.

⁶⁵ TNA, E 150/1161/13; C 142/140/203.

⁶⁶ *HMC Middleton*, 349.

⁶⁷ ibid. 370.

[68] UNMASC, Mi D 167.

[69] *HMC Middleton*, 416.

[70] ibid. 317.

[71] Clay, *North Country Wills*, 201.

[72] UNMASC, Mi 2/77/102.

[73] BIA 17184908

[74] *HMC Middleton*, 149, 560.

[75] TNA, E 150/1161/13; C 142/140/203.

[76] G. W. Marshall (ed.), *The Visitations of the Country of Nottingham in the Years 1569 and 1614* (1871), 181.

[77] *Visit. Notts.* 76; *HMC Middleton*, 511 See also TNA, STAC 2/24/182; C 1/412/56; C 2/Eliz./E2/36; C 43/2/34; C 146/11066; C 1/593/13 for further connections between John Egerton and the Willoughbys of Wollaton; UNMASC, biog. note on Sir Henry Willoughby.

[78] *Visit. Notts*, 28, 147; B. Burke, *The Grand Armoury*, (London), 1884, 660.

[79] e.g., UNMASC, Mi 1/3/1-2; Mi 5/169/84, 85, 88 dated 1562; Mi 2/77/102 ; Mi 6/175/68; *HMC Middleton*, 127, 515.

[80] BIA 17184908.

[81] TNA, PROB 11/28/534.

[82] UNMASC, Mi 6/176/190.

[83] Notts. Archives, DD/P/114/2.

[84] Folger Shakespeare Library, Cavendish-Talbot MSS, X d.428 (102).

[85] UNMASC, Mi C 15; HMC, *Middleton*, 152-5.

[86] Durant, *Bess*, 110, 126; Lovell, *Bess*, 292, 309.

[87] *HMC Middleton*, 542; J. A. M. Cruz, *An Account of an Elizabethan Family: The Willoughbys of Wollaton*, (Camden Series, 2019), n. 135. The author's suggestion that William's father may have been Henry Marmion cannot be correct. The writer of the 1582 Chatsworth letter says that he is going to consult his father and that his father was engaged in a dispute with Browne. Henry Marmion died on 4 January 1554.

[88] TNA, C 21/B10/3.

[89] *HMC Middleton*, 153-5.

[90] TNA, PROB 11/67/450.

[91] TNA, C 21/B10/3.

[92] BIA, Nottingham Act Book. Gabriel Marmion of Arnold, Admin, Jan 1590/1.

[93] UNMASC, 5/169/108-9; Ne D 848.

[94] BIA 17184976.

[95] TNA, C 21/B10/3.

[96] *The Records of the Honorable Society of Lincoln's Inn. Admissions and Chapel Registers,* The Honourable Society of Lincoln's Inn, (London), 1896, vol I, Admissions 1420-1799, 64; J. Foster, Grey's Inn Register of Admissions 1521 – 1889, 61-80; Inner Temple and Grey's Inn admissions online database http://www.innertemplearchives.org.uk/search; H.A.C. Sturgess (ed.), Register of Admissions to the Honourable Society of the Middle Temple, Vol I, (1949), 52-63.

[97] Durant, *Bess*, 117.

[98] UNMASC, Mi 6/170/124/5; Mi 5/169/1/104; Mi 5/169/1/108-109.

[99] *HMC Middleton*, 532-33.

[100] ibid, 550-51.

[101] ibid, 560-63.

[102] W. H. Stevenson (ed.), *Records of the Borough of Nottingham*, IV (1889), 417.

[103] UNMASC, Mi 5/169/1/105.

[104] Thomas Thurland married Robert Willoughby's daughter Jane, Visit. Notts. 148; *HMC* Middleton, 499. See for example *HMC Middleton*, 120, 455, 457.

[105] TNA, STAC 3/10/43 deals with an undated complaint made by Robert More against Ralph Egerton during the reign of Henry VIII. Among the defendants was a William Cooper. Ralph was the brother of Henry Marmion's wife, Isabel Egerton; *RBN,* 50, 419.

[106] The Clothing was the name given to the upper house of the town council of Nottingham at this period. Those who served the council in the office of bailiff or sheriff usually entered the ranks of the Clothing after their year of office. The town's seven aldermen were chosen from the ranks of the Clothing and the office of mayor of the town was generally rotated annually from among the ranks of the aldermen.

[107] *RBN*, IV, 409, 419.

[108] ibid, 179.

[109] ibid, 209, 202.

[110] ibid, 422.

[111] UNMASC, Mi 5/169/1/105.

[112] *RBN*, IV, 222.

7

Hardwick's Royal Princess:
Lady Arbella Stuart

Portrait of Arbella Stuart, attributed to Marcus Gheeraerts.
Reproduced by kind permission of the Earl of Strathmore and Kinghorne.

Arbella Stuart was the daughter of Charles Stuart, Earl of Lennox, and Elizabeth Cavendish. The exact date of her birth is uncertain. She was probably born in the autumn of 1575 at either Lennox House in Hackney or, possibly, at Chatsworth in Derbyshire. Her father was the younger brother of Henry Darnley, second husband of Mary, Queen of Scots, and father of the future James VI and I. Her mother was the daughter of Elizabeth, Countess of Shrewsbury, better known to history as 'Bess of Hardwick'.

Arbella's parents had been brought together by two formidable and ambitious women, Margaret Douglas, Dowager Countess of Lennox, and Bess of Hardwick. Neither had sought royal consent for the marriage and for her pains Margaret Douglas was to suffer her third spell in the Tower. The daughter of Henry VIII's sister, Margaret Tudor, Margaret Douglas was a granddaughter of Henry VII and first cousin to Elizabeth I. When Bess married her fourth husband George Talbot, Earl of Shrewsbury, in 1567/8 she was already a wealthy woman and ambitious for her six surviving children all fathered by her second husband, Sir William Cavendish. Arbella was niece to Mary, Queen of Scots, and first cousin of James VI of Scotland. She was the only English royal princess in the reign of Elizabeth I. Under English Common Law only someone born in England could inherit English land and/or succeed to the English throne. The law excluding foreigners from the English succession dated back to the reign of Edward III, a law which was, significantly, laid aside in 1604. Mary, Queen of Scots, and James VI were born in Scotland. In a letter of May 1578 to the Archbishop of Glasgow, Mary tried to circumvent the problem by stating that both she and her son, James, had been born "within the same isle". Furthermore, shortly before Mary was executed in February 1587 a new law stated that anyone descended from someone who had been found guilty of plotting against the crown could not succeed to the throne. In such circumstances there were many who came to believe that Arbella Stuart was the legal heir to the English throne.

Although Arbella was raised as a princess of the realm, whatever the ambitions of her grandmothers may have been, she was not to succeed to the crown. However, her story serves to illustrate the importance of the succession in early modern England. Following the fall of the Earl of Essex in 1601, Sir Robert Cecil's dominance at court ensured the succession of James VI of Scotland to the throne in 1603. Arbella's gender was not in her favour, had she been a man she may well have succeeded to the crown. Elizabeth's was a female court. During the reigns of the Tudor kings men had been accustomed to holding important and often lucrative court positions, such as that of Gentlemen of the Privy Chamber, which brought with them political power and status through which they could influence royal policy. This was not so in Elizabeth's court in which many such roles were given to women. Indeed, Elizabeth strictly forbade her court ladies to engage in matters of state. By the time Elizabeth's long reign drew to a close many powerful men had tired of a female court and wanted a return to the male dominated court life of Henry VIII and Edward VI. Despite his many years of service to Queen Elizabeth, William Cecil always believed that a king was preferable to a queen, a view shared by his son, Sir Robert Cecil. Bess of Hardwick was careful to maintain good relations with the Cecils. Although William Cecil had once championed the claims of the Greys and their offspring, by the 1590s both he and his son, Robert, chose to back the Stuart claim not in the shape of Arbella but in that of James VI of Scotland. Unlike Mary, Queen of Scots, Arbella did not have the support of English Catholics or powerful countries such as France or Spain. It is, however, doubtful that Arbella ever sought the crown or that Bess looked upon her granddaughter as Elizabeth's heir. Nevertheless, there were those who attempted to place Arbella on the throne.

Marriage became a major issue in Arbella's life. Any prospective husband would have had to have been of suitably high rank. Bess of Hardwick's fourth husband, George Talbot, Earl of Shrewsbury, claimed that Bess had tried hard to persuade him to seek a marriage for Arbella with almost every high-ranking family in England. In 1581, Elizabeth I considered marrying Arbella to Esmé Stuart (d 1583) but in 1583, at the age of eight, Arbella was betrothed to the three-year-old Lord Denbigh, son of Robert Dudley, Earl of Leicester. 'Little Robert', as he was known, died in 1584. Elizabeth also toyed with the idea of James VI as a potential husband for Arbella. As tensions with Philip II of Spain grew in the 1580s, in 1587 Elizabeth looked to marry Arbella to Rainutio Farnese, the son of the Duke of Parma, a proposal she revived in 1591. Possibly as a means of settling the dispute over the Lennox earldom, in 1588 and 1589 James VI proposed a marriage between Arbella and Esmé Stuart's son, Ludovic Stuart, Duke of Lennox, but this came to nothing. In 1590 rumour had it Arbella was to marry Henry Percy, Earl of Northumberland, and in 1596 Pope Clement VIII proposed Rainutio Farnese's brother as a husband for Arbella. In 1599 Robert Cecil suggested a match with Duke Mathias of Austria. The Prince of Condé, nephew to Henri IV of France, was considered in 1601 and in 1609 there were rumours of a marriage between Arbella and the Duke of Moldova.

Nothing ever came of these and other marriage proposals. Neither Elizabeth I or James I wanted Arbella to marry as her closeness to the English throne meant that children from a marriage could potentially become - as indeed Arbella was herself - rivals for the English throne. For much of her reign, Elizabeth I used the prospect of her hand in marriage as a political bargaining tool. As the queen aged beyond child-bearing years and her intention never to marry became obvious to all, this strategy became less viable. From the 1590s Arbella became a pawn in the Queen's foreign policy as a marriage with her was substituted for one with Elizabeth. After Elizabeth's death in 1603, James I had no more desire to see Arbella married than had Elizabeth before him and he ensured Arbella's dependence by depriving her of money and patrimony.

Arbella's father died the year after her birth. Up to the age of three and a half she was raised by her mother and paternal grandmother, Margaret Douglas. She first attended court at the age of three. After Margaret's death in 1578 Arbella, probably with her mother, moved to Chatsworth. She was well educated speaking six languages including Latin, Italian and French, and like Queen Elizabeth she wrote in an elegant italic hand. She studied the Bible and the classics, played the virginals and the lute, learned dancing and embroidery and, like other members of her family, became a skilled horsewoman. During her early years, time was spent with her cousins, the children of her aunt Mary, wife of Gilbert Talbot. Arbella's mother died in 1582 and Bess became her granddaughter's guardian. In 1587, at the age of twelve, Arbella returned to court. Possibly to annoy the Spanish, Elizabeth is said to have let it be known to the French ambassador that the day would come when Arbella would occupy the same position as Elizabeth herself. In 1588, Arbella became a Lady-in-Waiting to the Queen but was suddenly ordered back to Derbyshire to be kept under the watchful eye of her grandmother, Bess of Hardwick.

In 1603 the Venetian ambassador claimed that Arbella was dismissed from court by Elizabeth for seeking precedence over the other court ladies. There may have been some truth to this but the reminiscence came fifteen years after the event at a time when there were those at James I's court, including the ambassador himself, seeking to discredit Arbella. Another explanation for Arbella's abrupt removal from court is that this was the period of the Spanish Armada and there were fears she might be kidnapped and used as a figurehead by those seeking to replace Elizabeth as queen. Aged sixteen, Arbella returned to court with Bess in 1591 during the revived Farnese marriage proposals. It has also been suggested that in 1592 Arbella was ordered to leave the court by Elizabeth because she was rumoured to be close to the Queen's favourite, Robert Devereaux, Earl of Essex. Although Arbella's later letters suggest some kind of flirtation with the ill-fated earl, it is likely that Essex was merely using Arbella as a pawn in his own political intrigues. It is more likely that the discovery of a suspected plot to kidnap Arbella led the Queen to order her back to Derbyshire for her own safety. For the remaining eleven years of Elizabeth's reign Arbella was kept well away from court under the close supervision of her grandmother. When Elizabeth died on the 24th March 1603, Arbella was expected to lead the funeral procession but refused saying that the old Queen had not wanted her in life so she would not have her in death.

For much of her early adult life Arbella was more or less confined by her grandmother, Bess of Hardwick, in Derbyshire with no company of her own age and rank. It is said that at Hardwick New Hall she was eventually forced to sleep in the same bedchamber as her grandmother. In keeping a close eye on Arbella, Bess was merely following the instructions of the Queen and the Privy Council and, as the task grew more onerous, Bess more than once asked to be relieved of the responsibility. The move from the old hall into Hardwick New Hall took place in 1597 by which time Bess was in her seventies. Her view of the world had been shaped in the middle decades of the sixteenth century and as it drew to a close her attitudes would have doubtless seemed decidedly old fashioned and out-of-touch to Arbella, a young woman in her twenties who came to long for marriage as an escape from her enforced isolation. In late-1602, with no prospect of marriage in sight, Arbella came up with a scheme to marry Edward Seymour, the sixteen-year-old grandson of the ageing Earl of Hertford and his wife Katherine Grey (d.1568). The Grey sisters - Jane, Katherine, and Mary - were granddaughters of Henry VIII's sister, Mary. Arbella was the great-granddaughter of Henry VIII's sister, Margaret, and both she and the Grey sisters were descended from Henry VII. Why Arbella set her sights on Edward is unclear. It has been suggested that a match with the Seymours may have been considered at some earlier date.

Arbella seems to have developed an affinity with Lady Jane Grey, both women being ill- used by men seeking to put them on the throne in place of another. Hertford was the son of Protector Somerset and the nephew of

Queen Jane Seymour, mother of Edward VI. He had married Catherine Grey in 1560 but the marriage had taken place without the Queen's permission. Elizabeth had the marriage declared void and their two sons deemed illegitimate. Despite the taint of illegitimacy, under the terms of Henry VIII's will Edward had some pretention to the throne. Any offspring from a marriage to Arbella would have certainly had a very strong claim to the crown but having suffered greatly at Elizabeth's hands for his own marriage and fearful that a similar fate might befall his grandson the old earl immediately reported Arbella's scheme to the authorities.

Sir Henry Brounker, queen's commissioner, was sent to Hardwick by Sir Robert Cecil to investigate matters. In February 1603, Arbella again attempted an escape from Bess by declaring her real lover was not Edward Seymour but her cousin, James VI of Scotland. Brounker was again despatched to Hardwick. Both episodes can be seen as desperate attempts by Arbella to secure a release from confinement. In her efforts to persuade Brounker to recommend her removal from Hardwick, she penned lengthy, rambling depositions which became so badly scrawled as to be virtually illegible. At one stage she began a hunger-strike. Brounker's reports speak of Arbella's mood-swings, tantrums, busting into tears and saying all would be well if she could be released from her grandmother's care.

Having failed to convince Brounker to order her removal from Hardwick, Arbella became involved in an even more daring plan of escape. On the 10th of March 1603, her uncle, Henry Cavendish, and a company of armed retainers, rode up to the gates of Hardwick with the intention of rescuing Arbella. The ensuing commotion drew a crowd of astonished onlookers as Bess ordered the gates to be kept locked. From outside the walls Arbella could be heard creaming she was a prisoner. The whole affair ended in farce with Henry and his men riding away empty-handed. To what extent this attempt to secure Arbella's release was related to rumours of Elizabeth I's closeness to death is unknown but it seems likely. Sir Robert Cecil almost certainly saw it as part of a plan hatched by those against the Scottish succession and the remnants of the old Essex faction to place Arbella among 'friends' and it led to an investigation which saw Henry Cavendish summoned before the Privy Council.

Being so desperate to get away from Hardwick, it is possible that Arbella may not have been aware of the very grave position into which she had placed herself but Bess would have certainly recognised the dangers and it was at this time, in a letter to Sir Henry Brounker, dated that same 10 March 1603, that Bess was to describe Henry Cavendish as "my bad sonne Henry." There can be little doubt that Arbella's confinement with her grandmother had become unbearable. Arbella's later letters speak of how deeply she felt she had been misused by Bess. On the other hand, the situation must have been a very difficult and deeply frustrating one for Bess, torn, as she must have been, between her duty to the queen and the natural affection of a grandmother towards what she saw as a wilful and obstinate young woman whom she had raised from the age of seven.

Significantly, shortly before Elizabeth I's death, William Cavendish had Arbella moved to Oldcoates, a smaller property easier to defend than Hardwick's halls. He ordered muskets, powder and shot from London at the considerable cost of £80. Weapons and armour were also acquired from neighbours. Arbella was confirmed to the house under armed guard. William's most trusted servants were ordered to keep a lookout for any strangers arriving in the area. William clearly feared that another attempt would be made to secure Arbella's person by those opposed to James VI's succession to the throne of England.

The news of the old queen's death reached Hardwick within days and William rode into Chesterfield to hear James proclaimed king. A few weeks later William and his son attended on the new king at York. Arbella's fortunes seemed to improve with the death of Elizabeth I. King James was well aware of and had some sympathy for his cousin's plight. He ordered that she be allowed to leave Hardwick and be placed under the care of Henry Grey, Earl of Kent, at Wrest Park in Bedfordshire. By May 1603, Arbella, now aged 28 and still unmarried, was at court, and then housed at Sheen. It was at this time that two plots were discovered, the Main Plot and the Bye Plot. Not everyone was happy with the succession of the Scottish king to the English throne. In particular, the remnants of the defeated Essex faction resented the power that Cecil was now exercising under the new regime. The Bye Plot and the more serious Main Plot are little known, mainly because they have become overshadowed by the famous Gunpowder Treason of 1605. The Main Plot involved Lord Cobham and, allegedly, Sir Walter Raleigh. Its intended result was the assassination of King James and Sir Robert Cecil. Arbella was to be married to Lord Grey of Wilton and be placed on the throne. Henry Cavendish was implicated in the Bye Plot and ordered to appear before the Privy Council. It is possible that Arbella, however unwittingly, had come perilously close to involvement in something of a similar nature just two months earlier even though her only motive at that time had been to escape from Hardwick. She must have become aware, much as Bess herself had been aware, of the dangers of allowing herself to be manipulated by others as a rival for the crown for as soon as she had knowledge of the scheme, she herself reported the plot to Cecil. It is one of the great ironies that Arbella came to constitute such a threat to James in the same way that his mother had posed a threat to Elizabeth I.

Despite being on good terms with Queen Anne and her son, Prince Henry, a learned and serious-minded Arbella was to find she had little in common with the frivolities of James I's court. Yet her future, and this meant her marriage, was in the hands of her royal cousin. However, James, as already noted, had no more desire to see Arbella married than had his predecessor, Elizabeth I. Arbella may have been freed from what she saw as isolation and confinement at Hardwick but she was still not free to marry. In March 1605, she made a rare return to Hardwick. She had obtained an open letter from James I for the creation a peer of her choice and she knew full well that Bess would not be able to resist the temptation of acquiring the title of Baron Cavendish for her favourite son, Arbella's uncle, William Cavendish, even if it did come with a £2000 price tag. Bess had not wanted Arbella to come to Hardwick and Arbella herself was concerned about the kind of reception she would receive, so much so that she persuaded the king to write to Bess to smooth the way for the visit to take place. Bess questioned why someone who had so recently been desperate to be away from the place was now so desirous to return but, nevertheless, a degree of reconciliation did take place. Arbella left with gifts of a gold cup and £300 and was to be reinstated in Bess' will, the old countess dying on the 13th of February 1608.

By early 1609 Arbella, now in her middle thirties, was suspected of seeking a marriage with the Duke of Moldova but this was more likely a ruse to hide her renewed involvement with the Seymours, this time with Edward

Seymour's twenty-two-year old younger brother, William. Arbella was arrested and questioned about the Moldova marriage but in the end appears to have been under the impression that although James I would not favour a foreign match for his cousin he would look more favourably on a marriage to a loyal Englishman. She received an increase in her personal allowance and seemed to have returned to royal favour when, despite warnings from the Privy Council, she and William Seymour married secretly at 4 am on the morning of the 22nd of June 1610, a legal marriage but one which did not have royal consent. Some historians believe that at the time of these events James I may have suffered an attack of porphyria and that this helps explain his harsh treatment of the newly-weds. By the 8th of July, William was in the Tower and the next day Arbella was placed under house arrest in Sir Thomas Parry's house at Lambeth. James was determined to keep them apart probably to prevent any possibility of children whose claims to the English crown would potentially be greater than his own. A child from the marriage of Arbella and William would bring together the lines of Henry VIII's two sisters, Margaret and Mary Tudor. James decided to remove Arbella to distant Durham where she was to be placed in the custody of the bishop.

In March 1611, Arbella began the long journey north to Durham but did not get very far. The first night's stop was to be at Barnet but delays meant it was in fact spent at Highgate where Arbella apparently became ill. James sent one of his own doctors, Dr Hammond, to attend her. Hammond recommended she be moved to East Barnet where she was placed in the hands of Sir James Croft. Arbella's sickness, feigned or genuine, delayed the departure for Durham for almost twelve weeks. The king set a final deadline of Wednesday the 5th of June. James seems to have interpreted Arbella's actions as sheer obstinacy and was determined that he would be obeyed. He may have been intending to teach his wayward cousin a lesson for on more than one occasion Arbella was led to understand that after a short stay in the north the king's intention was to restore her to favour. She seems to have given little credence to such reports and, in any case, Durham was much too far away from her husband.

In an act worthy of a Shakespearian heroine, between two and three in the afternoon of Monday 3rd of June, Arbella left the house at East Barnet disguised in men's clothing, including rapier, and walked half a mile to an inn where horses were saddled and ready. By 6 pm she had ridden the 14½ miles to another inn at Blackwall where William was supposedly waiting, his luggage was there but there was no sign of the man himself. Boats were boarded to take Arbella and her party down river to a French ship which was to convey her and her husband to France but there was still no sign of William. Arbella spent the night in a boat and next morning boarded the French ship. She still wanted to wait for William but the captain insisted they sail otherwise the tide would be missed. William had made his escape from the Tower. Disguised in a black wig and beard, he had simply walked out of the West Gate following a cart but had set out later than planned and missed meeting up with the French ship and his wife. There was no contingency plan. William was able to find another ship and set sail but by this time their escape was known and James had sent ships after them. Arbella's ship lingered off Calais waiting for any sign of William but the ships that arrived were those sent by James with orders to arrest the Arbella and her husband and return them to England. Arbella was taken back to London and placed in the Tower. His first attempt thwarted by storms, William had by this time landed at Ostend and was to remain abroad until after Arbella's death. Once back in England he married Frances Devereaux, a daughter of the Earl of Essex, and within months was restored to royal favour. He was to name his eldest daughter, Arbella.

Languishing in the Tower, Arbella was yet again illegally deprived of her freedom. She was soon joined by her aunt Mary, Countess of Shrewsbury, who had master-minded the escape from East Barnet. In all, twelve people were arrested for their alleged part in the conspiracy. Arbella was never charged. It was enough for James that she had disobeyed him and all attempts to persuade him to release his cousin were ignored. Arbella's aunt, Mary, a known catholic, tried to persuade her to covert to the old faith. Instead, Arbella managed to obtain a copy of the key to her room and, rather than use it to escape, sent it to James I as a demonstration of her loyalty.

The death of James I's eldest son, Prince Henry on 6 November 1612 brought Arbella another step closer to the throne. The new heir Prince Charles was known to have health problems. In 1613 there appear to have been at least two plots to free Arbella from the Tower, one of which cost her the loss of several valuable pearls. Both plots, however, came to nothing. Arbella herself also seems to have conceived a scheme to fake the death and burial of William Seymour so that he could be brought to the Tower where husband and wife could live together in secret. In 1613, she entertained false hopes that she would be released to attend the marriage of James I's daughter, Elizabeth. As months of confinement turned into years of confinement, Arbella came to feel there would be no release. She took to her bed on 8 September 1614, she would either be released from the Tower or she would die there. Over the next twelve months, as Catherine Grey had done before her, Arbella refused medical attention and sustenance. Her health deteriorated and she died in the Tower on 25 of September 1615 at the age of just forty. There was to be no royal funeral but, on the king's order, her body was placed in the same Westminster Abbey vault as that of Mary, Queen of Scots, close to the coffin of James's son, Prince Henry.

There are those, both during Arbella's lifetime and since, who have argued that her actions betray a strain of madness. There is little doubt that as a young woman Arbella's desperate desire to marry, and through marriage escape what she saw as undue confinement in the hands of a woman who herself had had four husbands, produced periods of immense psychological stress that could easily have been interpreted as madness. Reading Brounker's reports Robert Cecil came to question Arbella's sanity but it suited his purpose to do so. He was already working to secure the succession of James VI to the English throne. Even though Cecil had probably concluded that she was not seeking the crown for herself, Arbella remained a potential threat to the success of his plans. In 1603, the Venetians reported that Arbella was, or was at least pretending to be, half mad but had their own reasons for doing so.

Arbella's bouts of so-called madness seem to have coincided with periods of extreme anxiety. Perhaps she suffered what in more recent times are referred to as stress related illnesses or 'nervous breakdowns'. Some historians have gone further by suggesting that Arbella was a victim of porphyria, a condition more famously associated with the alleged 'madness' of King George III, who was himself a descendant of James I. The disease has many symptoms including speedy recovery from bouts of mental instability, hysteria, vomiting, discoloured urine, sore eyes, and severe headaches to the front of the head. Other symptoms include diarrhoea, uncontrolled weeping, sensitivity to light, pain in the sides and weakness of the muscles. We should avoid the pitfall of assuming that anyone displaying such symptoms was necessarily a victim of the disease but Arbella's known symptoms do point to a possible diagnosis of variegate porphyria. Porphyria tends to be more prevalent in women of child-bearing age and was present in the Stuart line. James I and his mother, Mary, Queen of Scots, are thought by some to have suffered from the disease. It has been suggested that porphyria may have contributed to the death of James' eldest son, Prince Henry whereas Charles I does not seem to have displayed symptoms of the malady although his youngest daughter, Henrietta, may have been a sufferer as was her own daughter, Marie Louise, Queen of Spain. It has also been suggested that almost all descendants of King George III were afflicted by the disease and some medical historians argue that porphyria can be traced in the behaviour of Queen Victoria and a number of her descendants up to the present day. If porphyria was indeed the curse of the Stuarts how then did it get into Arbella's bloodline ? The mostly likely answer would seem to be via her paternal grandfather, Matthew Stuart, a descendent of James II of Scotland.

Was Arbella mad or simply misunderstood? Was she a victim of porphyria ? Perhaps we will never be sure for certain. It is well known that at the time of her death, Elizabeth I could not speak. Her deathbed was encircled by Cecil and members of the Cecil faction and, as the story goes, a list of possible successors was read out to the dying monarch and she raised her hand at the mention of James's name. We only have the word of those who were present when the old Queen supposedly signalled that James should succeed her to the throne. These men had a vested interest in securing the English throne for the Scottish king. What we do know is that the Duc de Sully, chief minister of Henri IV of France, who visited England in 1601, was to recall that it was common knowledge at that time that the English crown belonged rightfully to Arbella, a crown she was destined never to wear.

FURTHER READING:

Bradley. E. T., Life of the Lady Arabella Stuart: Containing a Biographical Memoir and a Collection of Her Letters, 2 vols, Kessinger Publishing, 2007.

Durant. David. N., Bess of Hardwick: Portrait of an Elizabethan Dynast, Weidenfield and Nicolson, London, 1978. Republished by Peter Owen, London, 1999.

Durant. David. N., Arbella Stuart: A Rival to the Queen, Weidenfield and Nicolson, London, 1978.

Gristwood. S., *Arbella: England's Lost Queen*, Bantam Books, London, 2003.

Hardy. Blanche, C., *Arbella Stuart: A Biography*, Kessinger Publishing, Legacy Reprints, 2010.
Reprint of a book first published in 1913.

Norrington. R., *In the Shadow of the Throne*, (Peter Owen), London, 2002.

Lovell. M. S., *Bess of Hardwick: The First Lady of Chatsworth*, 2005.

Steen. S. J., (ed), *The Letters of Lady Arbella Stuart*, O.U.P, Oxford, 1994.

Epilogue: My Bess

©National Trust images/John Bethall

My research is radically changing my view of Bess of Hardwick. By stripping away some of the long-held and oft repeated myths a very different picture emerges from that presented by previous authors.

Volume 3 of Sir William Dugdale's *An Historical Account of the Lives and most Memorable Actions of Our English Nobility* was published in the mid-1670s. Dugdale was writing around one and a half centuries after Bess's birth and some seven decades or so after her death by which time none of Bess's contemporaries were alive. Then, as now, very little was known about Bess's early life. Dugdale needed to explain how a woman from such a relatively undistinguished background as Bess ended her life as a countess whose wealth as a woman was reputedly second only to that of Queen Elizabeth I. This, of course, would not have been the case until the 1590s once Bess had acquired her Talbot dower. According to Dugdale,

Bess's four marriages brought her great wealth. He writes that Robert Barley's ...

"... great affections to her [i.e., Bess], she made such advantage; that, for lack of issue by her, he setled a large inheritance in Lands upon her self and her heirs; which, by his death, within a short time after, she fully enjoyed ..."

However, we know this was not the case. Dugdale goes on to tell us that Bess's marriage to Sir William Cavendish produced six surviving children. He skips over the fact that Sir William owed a huge sum to the crown at the time of his death and that Bess was left facing a parliamentary bill for the recovery of the debt and imminent destitution. Turning to the St Loe marriage Dugdale claims that Bess...

"... surviving Sir William Cavendish; and, discerning her self still youthful and amiable, and likewise courted by many; she made choice of Sir William St. Lo, Knight, (though much superior to her in years) then Captain of the Guard to Queen Elizabeth, and possessor of divers faire Lordships in Glocestershire. With whom she made such termes, in order to her Marriage with him, as that she fixt the Inheritance thereof, upon her self and her own heirs (for-fault of issue by him) excluding his own daughters and brothers..."

Dugdale here states that Bess's marriage to Sir William St Loe took place only on the condition set by Bess that he would leave his entire fortune to her. Dugdale was obviously aware that Sir William left his fortune to Bess but did not know the precise details and circumstances of that arrangement. Stating that Bess insisted on inheriting St Loe's fortune before she would agree to marry him served simply to support Dugdale's assertion that Bess '...became Mistriss of a very vast fortune, by her successful matching with several wealthy Husbands.' Turning to Bess's marriage to George Talbot, Dugdale tells us that she pulled off the same trick because Talbot ...

'... was captivated with her beauty; she stood upon such termes with him; that, unless he would yield; that Gilbert, then his second son, but afterwards his heir, should take Mary her daughter to wife; and that Henry her eldest

son, should marry the Lady Grace his youngest daughter; besides the setling of a large Joynture in Lands upon her self, he must not enjoy her. Unto all which he condiscending (and much more after) became her.'

It is difficult to accept the notion that a man like George Talbot, who did not need an heir, would have been allured by the 'beauty' of a 46-year-old thrice widowed woman who had borne the rigours of childbirth eight times in a single decade.

Reading Dugdale's view of Bess it becomes clear that within a few decades of her death the idea of her being a rapacious dynast was alive and well, laying the path for future commentators and biographers. In his manuscript *History of the Talbot Family* of 1692 the antiquary Nathaniel Johnson claimed he had been informed by two aged men that Bess met and married Robert Barley in London when both were in service to Lady Zouche of Codnor. Apparently, Johnson's informants told him that Bess attended and cared for a sickly Robert and the latter fell in love with and married her. Like Dugdale, Johnson claimed that Bess prevailed upon Robert Barley to settle his estate on her and her heirs such that after he died, she inherited a large estate. Those two aged men must have been exceptionally old to recall events that happened a century and a half previously. At best they could only have been providing Johnson with hearsay and the fact is we only have Johnson's word that he was told anything by anybody. We have already shown that Bess did not inherit a substantial estate from her first husband and there is no hard documentary evidence to prove that either Bess or Robert were ever in service to the Zouches or any other family. To complicate things further, there were two Lady Zouches at Condor at the time Bess was supposed to be in the family's service. Johnson's informants failed to identify exactly which Lady Zouche, Lady Anne or the aged Lady Margaret (neé Willoughby), they, and thus he, had in mind. Sir George Zouche and Anne Gainsford had only taken possession of Codnor in castle early in the 1540s. and may have been requiring additional household servants. The Zouches would have been considered an appropriate family of suitable rank in which Bess could be placed but this was also true of the Willoughbys and the Greys.

From Johnson let us turn our attention to Arthur Collins whose *Historical collections of the noble families of Cavendishe, Holles, Vere, Harley, and Ogle* was published in 1752. Following Dugdale's lead, Collins describes Bess as 'beautiful and discreet' and tells us that she married Robert Barley when she was fourteen years of age. When Robert died on the '2nd of February 1542 42 HVIII' Bess inherited his large estate. The 24th year of Henry VIII's regnal calendar ran from 22 April 1532 to 21 April 1533. Using New Style dating this means Collins dates Robert's death to February 1533. However, we know that Robert was born in January 1530 and died at the end of 1544. Furthermore, for Collins to be right Bess would have been born in 1519. In fact, the Barley inheritance passed to Robert's younger brother George and Bess was forced to struggle for several years through both Common Law and Equity Courts after Robert's death in order to secure her Barley dower. Collins goes on to tell us that Sir William Cavendish had a 'great affection' for Bess and that she simply had to use her charms to persuade him to relocate to Derbyshire and commence the building of Chatsworth. Like Dugdale, Collins tells us that Bess used her beauty, charm and wit, to captivate and beguile her husbands before conning them into handing over their inheritances. According to Collins Talbot was so smitten by Bess that she easily persuaded him to yield jointure to her and agree to the marriage of his son Gilbert to Bess's daughter Mary Cavendish. Collins wondered whether there had ever been a case for …

'... one woman to be four Times a happy and creditable Wife; to rise by every Husband unto greater Wealth, and higher Honours; to have an Unanimous Issue by one Husband only; to have all those children live, and all, by her Advice, be honourably, and creditably, disposed of in her Lifetime and, after all, to live Seventeen Years a widow, in absolute Power and Plenty.'

Dugdale and Collins present Bess as a consummate, calculating, confidence trickster. Putting aside the question of how feminine beauty was defined in the sixteenth century, we might ask why her husbands - or in this context victims - would have been so naive as to have fallen for such blatant trickery. It is hard to image men such as Sir William Cavendish, Sir William St Loe, and George Talbot, would have been so foolish. We have no images of a young Bess and one suspects neither did Dugdale. He had to come up with some explanation of how Bess had acquired her wealth and he did. Collins and later commentators simply followed suit. Oddly, Collins states that Bess became a widow for the fourth time on the 18th of November 1609, that is over a year and a half after her own death. He fails to note that two of Sir William's daughters by Bess did not reach adulthood. Collins also fails to recognise that, as we have seen elsewhere in this book, multiple weddings were a common feature among Elizabethan nobles, including the Talbots. If Bess was the driving force behind her daughter's marriage to Gilbert Talbot why did she not commemorate this marriage atop the Eglantine Table ?

Edmund Lodge published the second edition of his *Illustrations of British History* in 1838. In Volume II we are once again informed that Bess prevailed upon Robert Barley to settle his estate on her and her heirs. Lodge notes there was no issue from Robert's marriage to Bess such that the heirs who would ultimately benefit from this arrangement would be the offspring of a potential future marriage, in this instance Bess's marriage to Sir William Cavendish. Lodge repeats the story that Bess persuaded St Loe to sign over his inheritance to her but adds that this was 'to the utter prejudice of his two daughters by a former wife'. Bess then completed her 'conquests' by drawing Shrewsbury …

'… *into the same disgraceful and imprudent concessions which she had procured from his unlucky predecessors; and, partly by entreaties, partly by threats, induced him to sacrifice, in a great measure, the fortune, interest, and happiness, of himself and his family to the aggrandisement of her children by Sir William Cavendish* …'

However, we have evidence to show that William St Loe died without issue. The two daughters mentioned by Lodge were probably the children of Sir William Cavendish. I offer no apology for quoting in full Lodge's summation of Bess's character. She was, he says, …

'… *a woman of masculine understanding and conduct, proud, furious, selfish and unfeeling. She was a builder, buyer and seller of estates, a money-lender, a farmer, and a merchant of lead, coal and timber; when disengaged from these employments, she intrigued alternatively with*

Elizabeth and Mary, always to the terror and prejudice of her husband. She lived to a great old age, continually flattered, but seldom deceived, and died in 1607 [Old Style dating, 1608 New Style], immensely rich, and without a friend.'

Edmund Lodge re-hashed a good deal of what Dugdale, Johnson, and Collins had written. He added little to what was already known of Bess's marriages and repeated a good deal that was inaccurate. In his 1819 *Hallamshire* Joseph Hunter carried on where Edmund Lodge had left off, once more presenting Bess as a charmer and chancer who callously ruined her fourth husband.

We can demonstrate that all these accounts contain many fundamental errors. Therefore, we cannot take anything they say for granted or assume the accounts are accurate. Such authors set in train many of the myths that continue to appear in modern biographies and commentaries. Despite a degree of revision and rehabilitation, in one way or another, modern biographers persist with the view that Bess was a rapacious and unyielding dynast.

So, what about my Bess ? The weight of the evidence suggests that Bess was born into a minor Derbyshire gentry family around 1521/22. Those who maintain that she was born in 1527 fail to consider her legal proceedings for dower and the fact that her father provided funds for the upkeep of his daughters until each reached the age of 15. If 16 was the age of maturity for girls why did John Hardwick not provide for his daughters until they reached the age of 16 and why did Gabriel Marmion agree pay £40 to Anne Cooper's daughters when they attained the age of 19 ? Although John Hardwick's will refers to his daughters, they are not named individually. In the 1530s both Ralph Leche, Bess's stepfather, and close family associate Henry Marmion, claimed that they had purchased Robert Barley's marriage and wardship from Robert's father, Arthur Barley, probably with the intent of marrying Robert to one of John Hardwick's daughters, most likely Bess. The fact that at the time of their marriage Bess was some years older than 13-year-old Robert was neither unusual or important. Bess's marriage to Robert had nothing to do with love, as with most marriages in the sixteenth century, it was a typical business transaction between two north-east Derbyshire families of similar rank. This was not the last time Bess would find herself being used by men for their own ends. As an adult she was probably already literate and numerate but beyond this we have no evidence of the kind of education she may have received. Bess would have been over 21 when Robert Barley died. Ralph Leche may have been unwilling or unable to meet the cost of receiving Bess back into the household. This might explain why at this time Bess may have entered service in an aristocratic household.

Bess would have been brought up in the Catholic faith. Like Thomas Cromwell, the Greys and others of their circle, Sir William Cavendish came to favour evangelical Protestantism. Listed among his possessions at Northaw was an English Bible, probably Coverdale's 1539 Great Bible. Sir William St Loe, too, was a protestant. It may well have been during service in the Grey household that Bess was introduced to evangelical reform and turned away from the old religion. In her will, which she stated she had herself written, Bess speaks of the 'Elect', a term used principally by Calvinists and puritans.

No previous narrative of Bess has given sufficient treatment to the connections between the Hardwicks, the Willoughbys and their servants, the Marmions. Bess herself first appears in the historical record in 1528 as an unnamed daughter in her father's will. In 1543/4 Peter Freschevile alleged that Bess's stepfather, mother, and family associate Henry Marmion, had forcibly abducted Robert Barley and that Bess's undated marriage to Robert was illegal. We have the complaint Bess made to Chancery in 1546 which gives some details of her marriage to Robert and of her efforts to secure dower. If Bess did go into service within an aristocratic household following the death of her first husband, she would have witnessed the type of education received by noble children, especially if she was service to the Greys. She would also become aware of the furnishings, tapestries, and trappings, typical of Tudor aristocratic households. A perusal of sixteen century aristocratic inventories readily demonstrates a propensity for French furniture, Turkey carpets, fine fabrics, hangings and tapestries. Bess's marriage to Cavendish introduced her to a wider circle of county families, some of high standing. It also provided her with higher rank and the opportunity to become mistress of a household, a role in which she could put into practice what she had imbibed. She may have acquired or perhaps developed her well-known accounting skills under Sir William's tutelage. At this stage of her life, Bess was no more than the dutiful wife a man of Cavendish's rank and profession could expect. In his Star Chamber action against the 1548 enclosure rioters he referred to Bess only as his wife, not by name, and he made no refence to her having at the time been some eight months pregnant with their first child. Pregnancy was nothing new to Sir William, after all he was considerably older than Bess. He had already fathered eight children and was no stranger to childbirth.

Bess's marriage to St Loe brought relief from the burden of Cavendish's debts together with the means to continue with the building of Chatsworth. We know from various inventories that Bess appears to have furnished properties in a fashion appropriate to her rank. We need to be cautious when ascribing any particular empathy or affinity she may or may not have had with styles, themes, or characters, as these would have been found in almost any aristocratic household of the Elizabethan renaissance. In later life, Bess was happy to purchase pre-owned tapestries and to copy architectural features she had seen elsewhere. Hardwick new hall was originally intended to have had a double stairway but Bess appears to have abandoned this in favour of a grand winding staircase leading to the High Great Chamber after having seen that which Sir Christopher Hatton had installed at his magnificent house at Holdenby, Northamptonshire. The High Great Chamber frieze at Hardwick is a rare survival of Elizabethan architecture but William Cecil had such a frieze at Theobalds with trees so realistic it was said birds built their nests in them, a conceit that would have delighted the Elizabethans. We know that Bess's son Charles Cavendish saw this frieze. The building of Hardwick's new hall had probably already extended above the height of the second floor when in 1592 Bess purchased Hatton's Gideon tapestries. Typically, the State Rooms of an Elizabethan prodigy house would be located on the second floor. I suspect that the height of the Gideon tapestries was too great for them to hang on the second floor. This led to a reversal of the norm with the State Rooms being placed on the third floor the height of which was constructed to accommodate the Gideon tapestries. In order to maintain the symmetry of the building this in turn necessitated the addition of a further mullion to Hardwick's towers.

EPILOGUE: MY BESS

The death of Sir William Cavendish must have had a traumatic and lasting effect on Bess, not simply due to the loss of another husband but also due to the stress created by the situation in which she found herself. For the second time she was on the cusp of destitution but now with six children to support. This may have been a significant turning point in her life. Her struggle for her Barley dower and renewed fears of debt and poverty following the death of Sir William Cavendish may have driven her to crave financial security for herself and her children. She was fortunate to have a good friend in Sir William St Loe who came to her rescue. They had known each other for many years before they married. He was certainly not desperate for an heir as some have claimed. Had that been the case he would have remarried long before 1559. He and Bess spent relatively little time together during their six years of marriage. I find it hard to accept the idea that Queen Elizabeth demanded his attendance at court merely to spite Bess. I doubt that there was ever any intention for them to live together. Modern notions of love and marriage have little place in Tudor England. The fact that St Loe entrusted his inheritance to Bess had more to do with the complete breakdown of his relationship with his brother than it had to do with Bess. Bess had managed to escape impending poverty and destitution and she would have been determined never to find either herself or any of her children in such straits in the future.

My Bess was not a confidence trickster or an ambitious dynast. I do not believe that she harboured a nefarious determination to fleece each of her husbands in turn. Irrespective of the advantages it might bring, I don't see Bess's marriage to George Talbot as the result of a single-minded quest for a title. Her brother James had greatly increased the size of the family estate at Hardwick but had virtually bankrupted himself in the process. In 1584 Bess's son William purchased the Hardwick estate on his mother's behalf, a fortuitous purchase which came at a time when Bess's marriage to George Talbot had completely broken down. She had had to leave Chatsworth and needed to find a new home. This must have been another stressful period for Bess and may well have revived fears of debt and poverty. We tend to think of stress as a modern ailment but recognisable symptoms of stress can be seen in the lives of Bess, Arbella, Robert Devereaux, Sir Walter Raleigh, Mary, Queen of Scots and many more. During the sixteenth-century, unprecedented inflation led many nobles, including George Talbot, to turn from the traditional way of gaining their incomes from copyholds, long-term fixed rents, and entry fines, to short-term leaseholds and rack-renting. Some, notably George Talbot, began the commercial exploitation of their estates and the resources they contained such as coal, iron, timber, pasture for sheep and cattle and warrens and fishponds. Bess's sons William and Charles would have learned from Shrewsbury's example and did much to increase the extent and income of the Hardwick estate.

In the Introduction to this book I warned readers that they might find some of my views challenging, controversial and, yes, even heretical. My Bess is a woman of her time, in many ways unexceptional. She certainly should not be lauded as a proto feminist. The sixteenth century produced many outstanding women: Margaret Willoughby, Anne Stanhope, Elizabeth Brooke, Margaret Lennox, Lettice Knollys, Penelope Rich, and the Cooke sisters to name just a few, but all were products of their time. I have little doubt that over the centuries much has been attributed to Bess that rightly ought have been credited to others. My Bess is more human than she is often portrayed. Subject to human frailties, she was just as often at the mercy of events as she was controlling them. Sometime soon someone will publish a new biography which considers recent research and provides its readers with a scholarly revision of Bess of Hardwick. Such a book is badly needed.

FOR THOSE WHO WISH TO PERSUE THIS FURTHER:

For Dugdale's *Baronage* go to http://tei.it.ox.ac.uk/tcp/Texts-HTML/free/A36/A36794.html

Arthur Collins's *Historical collections of the noble families of Cavendishe, Holles, Vere, Harley, and Ogle* is available at ancestry.uk

For Edmund Lodge's *Illustrations of British History* go to https://archive.org/details/abj0212.0001.001.umich.edu/page/XXVIII

There is a copy of Nathanial Johnson's *History of the Talbot Family* at Chatsworth House.

P Riden and D Fowkes, *Hardwick a great house and its estate*, (Phillimore, Chichester) VCH, University of London, 2009.

READERS NOTES